UNIX

The Minimal Manual

PRINCIPLES OF COMPUTER SCIENCE SERIES

Series Editors

Alfred V. Aho, *Bell Telephone Laboratories, Murray Hill, New Jersey*
Jeffrey D. Ullman, *Stanford University, Stanford, California*

Theo Pavlidis
Algorithms for Graphics and Image Processing

C. K. Wong
Algorithmic Studies in Mass Storage Systems

David Maier
Theory of Relational Databases

Jeffrey D. Ullman
Computational Aspects of VLSI

Narain Gehani
Advanced C: Food for the Educated Palate

Narain Gehani
C: An Advanced Introduction

Narain Gehani
C for Personal Computers: IBM PC, AT&T PC 6300, and Compatibles

Leonard R. Marino
Principles of Computer Design

Christos Papadimitriou
The Theory of Database Concurrency Control

Michael Andrews
Computer Organization

Steven Tanimoto
Elements of Artificial Intelligence Using LISP

Egon Börger, Editor
Trends in Theoretical Computer Science

Martti Mäntylä
An Introduction to Solid Modeling

Jeffrey D. Ullman
Principles of Database and Knowledge Base Systems, Volume I

Jim Moore
UNIX: The Minimal Manual

OTHER BOOKS OF INTEREST

Arto Salomaa
Jewels of Formal Language Theory

Jeffrey D. Ullman
Principles of Database Systems

Kurt J. Schmucker
Fuzzy Sets, Natural Language Computations, and Risk Analysis

Stuart C. Shapiro
LISP: An Interactive Approach

UNIX
The Minimal Manual

Mail
Files and Directories
Word Processing:
Editing, Formatting and Printing
and
Automatic Bibliographies

JIM MOORE

COMPUTER SCIENCE PRESS

Library of Congress Cataloging-in-Publication Data

Moore, Jim, 1950–
UNIX : The Minimal Manual Jim Moore.
p. cm.
Includes index.
ISBN 0-7167-8195-6
1. UNIX (Computer operating system) I. Title.
QA76.76.063M65 1988 88-29943
005.4 – 3—dc19 CIP

Printed in the United States of America

Computer Science Press, Inc.
1803 Research Boulevard
Rockville, MD 20850
An imprint of W.H. Freeman and Company
41 Madison Avenue, New York, NY 10010
20 Beaumont Street, Oxford OX1 2NQ, England

1 2 3 4 5 6 7 8 9 0 RRD 7 6 5 4 3 2 1 0 8 9

This is a different sort of Unix systems book.

The Minimal Manual does not assume you know *anything* about computers.

The Minimal Manual does not assume you *want* to know anything about computers.

The Minimal Manual simply tells you how to get things done on your computer.

Simply.

Quick Contents

Long Table of Contents

Acknowledgments

Although, to be truthful, this book is largely mine in not only the germination and writing, but also in design and layout of the text, it has, even so, had the attentions of others who have helped to make it better.

First and foremost, there is my wife, Nancy M. Tanner, who, in her capacity as a doctor of anthropology at the University of California, was given a terminal and an account on a computer system that used UNIX. The instructions provided were nearly incomprehensible. This act introduced me to the need for a simplified manual for UNIX that didn't confuse the beginning UNIX user, or insult their intelligence. A "minimal" manual. Nancy suggested I write up this simpler manual as a book, and she also edited the first drafts. She's helped and supported me immeasurably during the process of producing a finished product from blank screen and paper.

Barbara and Arthur Friedman from Computer Science Press, with the help of their series editors, Jeffrey Ullman of Stanford University's Computer Science Department and Alfred Aho from Bell Labs, were sharp enough to spot the book as a well thought out concept (obviously I concur). They, along with the folks from W.H. Freeman, showed rare talent in being able to help in its execution without stepping on the basic conceptual design.

At W.H. Freeman, Project Editor Diane Maass, Senior Copywriter Jim Borghoff, and Art Director Mike Suh have worked hard and well to bring the book through the final push to production. Alan Gold did the final copy editing and I found his suggestions so good I used probably 95% of them. He also had that nice style of suggesting a change without making you feel like a dunce for making a mistake. There are many others whom I do not know who have worked and will work on **UNIX: The Minimal Manual**, and I thank them all.

Last I'd like to thank some folks who are often forgotten at times like this: my elementary school teachers from Holmes School in Rochester, Minnesota. They taught me something when I was very young that I've never forgotten, and always find useful: It's not so important to memorize something as to know where to look it up. For people who are using UNIX: **The Minimal Manual** is where to look it up.

Chapter 1

The Minimal Manual: Introduction to Unix

Unix has been touted as a system that will be around for a long time. It will. The Unix system is also supposed to be incredibly difficult to learn. It isn't. **The Minimal Manual** makes the Unix system easy to learn and easy to use. Just remember these three points and a Unix system really **can** make your work easier.

1. You don't need to know **anything** about computer programs to run a computer.

2. All you need to learn is what commands to use to make the computer do what you want it to do.

3. Forget those ads threatening that your four-year-old kids will be lost in the future if they don't know how to program computers.

You Don't Have to Learn to Be a Plumber to Take a Shower.

This manual is by far the best buy in Unix manuals. If you don't believe me, just look at any of the others. The commands covered in this book are found on almost all versions of Unix – for any command I describe that isn't on every Unix system I also describe a simple way to tell if your Unix system has it. I don't try to impress you with arcane facts, figures, and techniques for Unix systems. I'm simply showing you how to use a very good system that has been poorly explained.

The Minimal Manual doesn't present you with a smattering of everything there is to know about Unix systems. It tells you in detail how to *use* Unix, how to use the electronic mail, make files and directories to organize your writing, use the editing and formatting systems, and print out the results. These are basic features that everyone uses, from novice to expert.

Both novices and experts who are new to Unix systems will find this book useful because it covers basic features – and covers them in enough detail to make it possible to work with the computer without having to search through any other books. I deliberately *don't* get into features that some use and some don't, such as programming. And I make it easy to look up information about commands, so you can use **The Minimal Manual** as a reference while you work.

Most of this book is in two columns. The descriptions of commands are in the left side column; the commands are in the right one. This is how novices usually find the commands they want, using a natural reading style – from left (**description**) to right (**command**). As you remember more commands, you may find it quicker to search for a command first, then double-check the description to make sure it does what you thought it did. Since the commands are not buried in blocks of text, this is easy to do. The text that spans both sides of the page has been kept to a minimum; it introduces you to the various sections and gives warnings. There aren't that many warnings, because computers are really not very hard to use.

People who use Unix systems tend to fall into one of two wildly divergent categories: certifiable computer experts and complete novices. Experts will probably find that the beginning of each chapter covers basic information they already know. They can skip over this basic information and go right to the commands without offending me in the slightest. For instance, right now, so that the novices won't feel lost, I'll explain simply and thoroughly what equipment they will be using. Experts can skip right over most of this chapter and touch down at the last section, **Give Commands to Your Computer**. That section explains the conventions used in **The Minimal Manual** to indicate the prompt, return and control keys, and spacebar. If you don't know what a prompt or control key is, you're a novice and should read the whole chapter. It's not long.

Learning Unix

Now that the experts have left for the back of the chapter, let me reassure you that there are huge numbers of Unix novices out there. You are not alone. Maybe I should say "we," because everyone is a novice sometime. I was, and I make a point of remembering it, because that helps me help you learn the Unix system in a non-scary way. Trust me – if you are approaching a computer for the first time, your first step should be **don't worry about it**. Using a computer is *not* always easy, but it's not *really* hard, either, and it gets easier all the time. As it gets easier, your work gets easier, too. Some of you may even find it fun. Those that don't find it fun will still find it very useful.

If you want to use a computer for writing and editing or rearranging a text, making bibliographies that can be alphabetized with a simple command to the computer, printing out what you've written, or formatting the pages so they look nice, this manual is what you need. If you want to use the computer to do graphics and programming, this manual will provide the bridge you need to be able to understand the Bell System Manuals and other books that attempt to teach those more complex subjects. The question is, do you want to *use* the computer to accomplish a task, or do you want to wade through a swamp of information until you reach enlightenment? If you want to go through the swamp, this manual will put you on the right path; if you want only to be able to use the computer to make your writing and editing easier, you can step off the path at any time. I'll leave you on solid ground.

Unix is a nice computer system with a strong oral tradition, reinforced by technical, jargon-filled, and unnecessarily wordy manuals – in the technical, jargon-filled, and unnecessarily wordy world of computers these are called "user documentation." Most of the oral and written instruction so far devised for Unix systems has assumed that you want to know *everything* about Unix, and right away. If you could look at the account names of the people using your computer system and what they are doing (which you can do on some Unix systems, using a **w** command), you'd find most of them using mail, editing, formatting, and printing. These are computer functions even the programmers use; they are basic, and that's why I teach them in this manual. Most people don't want to *make* programs; they want to *use* programs. They use programs, such as editing and formatting, because these programs can make their work easier. A Unix system really *can* make your work easier.

Look back at the table of contents and see what you want to learn to do with your computer. Except for logging in and out (connecting and disconnecting), *everything* is optional. Never let anyone make you feel guilty because you have more important things to do than learn how to do something on a computer! Learn what *you* want to learn. Ignore the rest.

What Is a Unix Computer System?

And what's in one?

Some personal computers are using Unix systems now, and its use will become more common as small computers are designed with more and more memory. However, the Unix system is usually associated with medium-sized and large computers that are often placed at a central location and connected to terminals through cables or phone lines. So what makes up a typical Unix system?

There's a **terminal**. That's what most people think of as a computer. You've undoubtedly seen the elements of a terminal. It consists of a keyboard (like a typewriter's, with a few extra keys) and a monitor (a TV-type screen). Your terminal needs to be plugged into a wall socket, like a lamp. It needs to be connected to the computer, either directly (''hard-wired''), or remotely, over phone lines via a modem.

There may be a **modem**. You only need a modem if you are going to want your terminal to communicate with the computer over phone lines instead of directly. If you are using a modem, it needs to be connected to your terminal through a special cord that plugs into a socket marked ''(RS232),'' which computer designers usually put around in the back of the terminal to make it hard to get at. Your modem needs to be plugged into a wall socket, too.

There will be a **computer**, somewhere. If you are dealing with a small personal or micro computer, the computer will be right there with your terminal. On most Unix systems, the computer is off somewhere behind a locked door so it can't get out. It's probably in the basement if you want to go look at it. Computers are often kept locked up where they (and their keepers) can stay away from lightning, fire, earthquakes, thieves, and people who ask too many questions.

The computer also has to be plugged in, but if it's off in the basement somewhere, you don't have to do it.

There's probably a **printer** or two. A printer is basically a heavy-duty, high-speed typewriter without keys. It doesn't have to be near your terminal or even in the same building. It just has to be hooked up to the main computer and is usually somewhere near it.

And each printer has to be plugged in.

In the computer there must be memory. A computer is literally nothing without its memory. Everything a computer is to be told to do must be in its memory. A command given to a computer is shorthand for a more complicated set of instructions the computer follows explicitly. These machines would be incredibly slow to use if it wasn't for the fact that the computer follows its instructions at almost the speed of light. At the speed of electricity, actually. If the computer's memory is faulty, it cannot find or follow instructions. It cannot find your files. It cannot function. It cannot help you. That's why a Unix system uses three stages of memory retention: the **buffer**, the **disk**, and the **tape**. You see...

...the memory in the computer goes round and round...

In the **buffer** electricity runs around in microscopic circles, turning microscopic switches on and off like a crazy monkey – but in carefully controlled patterns. When you are typing at your terminal, you are dealing with the buffer.

For longer-term memory those patterns are ''written to the **disk**.'' The disk looks like an enclosed record player; it works rather like a very accurate tape recorder. This is where your files usually are; the disk makes them easy to get at and keeps them relatively safe. Power outages can't get at your files, although headcrashes can. That's when the recording head touches the disk and gouges out bits of somebody's files – probably yours.

Because of headcrashes, on most systems the files are periodically ''dumped'' onto a **tape**. They are harder to get at, but at least they're safe. You don't have to do anything special to dump your files; it's taken care of by the ''system administrators.'' You don't have to worry about it.

Give Commands to Your Computer

Don't pussyfoot around. It's there to help you, and you control it.

The **prompt** is a symbol the computer displays on the terminal's screen. A Unix system prompt is usually a **$** or **%**, and it's there to let you know that the computer is ready to accept a command from you. **Chapter 10, Hidden Files**, shows you how to change the prompt to something more personal, such as "YOUR COMMAND, PLEASE:" or "WHAT DO YOU WANT FROM ME? I'M JUST A STUPID COMPUTER." You can make your computer say anything you like. *You* are in charge. Just type the commands the way I show you, and you'll find that the Unix system *is* easy.

In **The Minimal Manual**, some parts of commands, such as *filename* or *line number*, are italicized. This means you should type whatever file name or line number you want in that space. The rest of the command is in boldface so that you can easily see exactly what you need to type.

When you are supposed to push the **RETURN** key or hold down the **CONTROL** key, I show this as **[RET]** or **[CTRL]**.

You push the **RETURN** key *after* you give a command so that the computer will know that it should carry out the command. After the computer has carried out that command, it shows it is ready to carry out another by displaying the prompt.

When you use a **CONTROL** function, you hold down the **CONTROL** key *while* you type a command letter. The **CONTROL** key works like a typewriter's shift key, but instead of printing the letter in uppercase it makes that letter's key perform some other function and doesn't print anything at all. Common **CONTROL** key functions are **[CTRL]i** for *indent*, **[CTRL]c** for *cut that out!* (it stops the present operation and makes the computer ask you for another command), and **[CTRL]s** for *stop!* (it stops the printout on the screen until you restart it by hitting the **[SPACEBAR]**).

Chapter 11 contains **Emergency Relief**. It explains things, like the **[CTRL]c**, that will help you out if the computer keeps running on and doesn't want to respond to reason.

Chapter 2

Logging In and Out

Before you **log in**, or connect up to the computer, you need to have your terminal plugged in and hooked up. If you are sharing a system with other people (a multi-user system), you also need to get an account from your computer center or administrator. The center administrator will tell you whether you need a modem or if you can use a hard-wire connection.

A hard-wire connection will allow your terminal to react faster and won't tie up your phone line when you are using the computer. This setup may be found in an office where a lot of people are using computer terminals hooked up to the main system. A system using a modem can be used anywhere you can plug in a phone. Your computer center will tell you the telephone number to call to let your terminal talk to the computer. To use a modems you just make sure your modem and phone are plugged into their respective outlets and put the phone handset into the modem. Newer modems don't utilize the phone handset; they just plug into the phone jack in the wall.

If you are using a hard-wire connection, all you need to do is switch the terminal on. As soon as it warms up, a little rectangle or blinking line will appear on the screen. This is the **cursor**, and it shows your position on the screen. If nothing happens at all, double-check all the connections. If they are okay and still nothing happens, something may be broken. Sorry, that's another book.

Now you can log in and start using your computer.

When you get your account, you'll also get an account name and a temporary password. You can keep that password but will probably want to change it so that nobody else can use your account – how to change your password is in the next section. If you are going to use a remote system, you will also get a phone number to call to hook your modem up to the main computer.

If you are hard-wired, just hit the **RETURN** key to get started: **[RET]**

If you are using a remote system with a modem, hook your phone up and dial the phone number you got from the computer center: *phone number*

If you had listened to the phone instead of plugging it into the modem, when the computer answered you would have heard a high-pitched tone. It's music to the computer's ear.

Since some systems have more than one computer, the exact words your computer uses when you log in may vary slightly.

If there is more than one computer on your system, the computer will ask something like: WHICH COMPUTER?

You type the letter or number or name of the computer you have an account on;

then hit the **RETURN** key (**[RET]**):	*computer name or number* **[RET]**
The computer may say something like:	Go
You hit the **RETURN** key again:	**[RET]**
The computer will print some gobbledegook and stop. You may have to hit the **RETURN** key several times until the computer prints:	Login:
You answer with your login (account) name, followed by **[RET]**:	*your account name***[RET]**
Then it will ask for your password:	Password:
Type in your password. Because you want to keep it secret, it won't show up on the screen when you type it, but the computer will read it anyway. Follow with **[RET]**:	*password* **[RET]**
If you mistyped your login name or your password, the computer will tell you by saying:	Login incorrect
or by saying:	Password incorrect

Then it will ask for your login name and password again, just as before. Try again.

If you forget your password or login name, you will have to go to the people you got your account from and go through that process again. Don't be embarrassed. It happens.

If you got your login name and password correct, the computer will run a few lines by you and then ask you what type of terminal you are using so that it can adjust its responses to account for keys in different positions and such. It may say:

TERM (adm3a)

Or perhaps:

TERM (tvi912)

Your computer center or system manager should be able to tell you what to call your terminal. Usually it's an abbreviation of the terminal model name. If your terminal type is the same as what the computer asked you, just hit **[RET]**:

[RET]

If it is different, type in the terminal type, for instance:

tvi925[RET]

Now the computer will display some more stuff for your edification. If you don't want to be edified, just ignore it. It may tell you:

You have mail

In the next chapter I explain mail.

Or it may show you some messages from the computer center and ask whether you want to read them.

If you want to read the message, say *yes*:

y[RET]

If you don't, say *no*:

n[RET]

If you want to skip the messages and get

on to something else, *quit*: **q[RET]**

If you use **q** to stop looking at messages, the ones you didn't see will show up the next time you log in.

Now you are ready to do whatever you wanted to do on the computer.

Changing Your Password

You can change your password by yourself. No one has to know what it is. Here's how you do it: % **passwd[RET]**

% is the computer's prompt. You don't need to type %.

The computer will check to see if it should let you do this by asking you to type your present password: Old password:

Type your present password: *your present password* **[RET]**

Then the computer will ask you to type your new password: New password:

Type your new password: *your new password* **[RET]**

Now the computer will ask you to retype it: Again

This is to be sure you typed it correctly. Since you can't see the password as you type it, you should be very careful as you do this: *your new password* **[RET]**

Your password is well protected by a code system, so you are the only one who knows it unless you talk in your sleep or let people read it over your shoulder. If you forget your password, you will have to go to your system administrator and go through the process of getting a new account and retrieving your files. This will take some time, so try not to lose it.

Logging Out

Logging out is simple.

If you're *done*, just type: % **[CTRL]d**

Or type: % **logout[RET]**

The computer will print some message or other and disconnect itself.

Chapter 3

Mail

This is a good first step if you are on a system with other people, especially friends. You can send mail to them, and if you're lucky, you'll get some back. Enjoy it while you can; they'll have junk mail on these things before you know it.

To read your mail:	% **Mail[RET]**
The system will go through some rigamarole and then tell you if you have any mail, and how much, like this:	2 messages, 2 new
Hit **[RET]** and it'll also tell you who sent them, using their account names, for instance:	hambo
Just type the number of the letter you want to read first, and it will be printed:	**1[RET]**
After you've read it, you may want to *save* it. If so:	s *filename*[**RET**]

If you want to *delete* (get rid of) it:	**d[RET]**
If you want to *quit* reading your mail and do something else, type:	**q[RET]**

This will bring you back to the real world; that is, it will take you out of mail mode. Sometimes you will get stuck in the never-never land inside your computer and won't know how to get out. You'll start believing in *Alice in Wonderland* and even *Tron.* Don't worry; there's a chapter in this book (**Chapter 11**, appropriately) called **Emergency Relief** that can get you out of such scrapes. You might want to flip back there and take a look just to reassure yourself that **help** is at hand.

Sending Mail

If you know someone's account name (or "accountname," as the computer reads it), you can send that person a letter. I'll show you how.

To send mail to someone who is on your computer system, just type:	% **Mail** *accountname***[RET]**
The computer will reply:	Subject: *you can write anything here – it's just like a title* **[RET]**
Then you type the body of the letter as if you were using a typewriter. When you're *done* typing and ready to send it, type a **[CTRL]d** on a line by itself:	**[CTRL]d**
Hold down the **[CTRL]** key while you type **d**.	
The computer will ask if you want to send a copy to anyone else by saying:	Cc:
You can send a copy to anyone else you like (or if it's a nasty letter, to anyone you don't like). It's handy to send a	

copy to yourself so that you can keep it in your files. Just type in the account name:

accountname

If you want to send copies to two or more people, just type their account names one after the other, leaving a space between each one:

accountname accountname

After you type in the account name(s), just hit:

[RET]

and it's on its way.

When you get the account name wrong or otherwise mess up, your mail will come back to you via the "Mail Daemon." Sorry, try again. But check the account name first.

Mailing Files

After you start making files, you may want to send a copy of one of your files to someone. To do this, type:

% **Mail** *accountname* <*filename* **[RET]**

and off it goes.

The "greater than" (>) and "lesser than" (<) symbols are used a lot with files. They are often called redirects by computer folks because they act like arrows indicating that something be put in a file (>*filename*) or a copy be taken out (*filename* <).

Also please note that you can leave spaces between the the command, the <, and the *filename* **or** you can leave out either of the spaces around the <. It won't matter; the command will work just the same.

If someone has mailed you a long file (or if you mailed one to yourself from another machine) you may not want to read it all when you get it in the mail. But (presumably) you want to save it. Just start reading it (using the commands described at the beginning of this chapter), and while it is printing on your screen, tap: **[CTRL]c**

The message will stop in a little while. Then you *save* it in a file by typing: s *filename* **[RET]**

This way you don't have to read the whole file before you can save it.

Mail to Other Computers and Other Places

When you're hooked up to one of the fancy systems, you can send mail to people who aren't on the same computer with you if you know how to route it. You just need a more complete address to go with the account name. The computer should have a file to help you out with this sort of thing. Try asking the computer's help file for assistance. **Chapter 9, Help from the Computer**, shows you how to do this. If the computer doesn't have this information, ask your computer center. Maybe your boss doesn't want anyone to know the info, figures employees will pass notes all day. If so, find a computer nut (sixties lingo), a computer freak (seventies), or a computer geek (eighties), and ask them how to do it. Don't let your boss get away with it; it's not called it an information *revolution* for nothing.

Be sure to get an explanation in plain English rather than computerese. Better yet, have them write the instructions down.

The basic form is:

% **Mail** *accountname*@-*machinename* **[RET]**

If the person you want to reach is on your own system, the account name and machine (computer) name should be enough of an address. If they are on another, more remote system, you need to append a longer address to the back of *machinename*. At the present state of the art, you need to get the computer address (often called email address) from the person you want to send mail to.

Chapter 4

Files and Directories

Files contain your notes and writings. Directories can only contain files and other directories. It's good to make different directories to separate different subjects or articles. After you've made a number of files, it can be hard to remember what you've written in each. Having your files separated according to subject keeps you from getting too confused. If you have one directory named MANUALS and another named COMPUTER.LITERACY, you can use the same file names in each directory (such as draft1, draft2, index, etc.) and not get the files' contents confused.

Files and directories branch off each other like a tree, and you can keep branching them off ad infinitum if you have enough storage space in the computer. You'll start off in your *"Home Directory,"* the place you first enter when you log in and your starting point for building a network of files and subdirectories. The figure on the next page shows you what a diagram of your files and directories might look like.

File Names

File and directory names can be any combination of letters and/or numbers up to a total of fourteen. That's the standard Unix system explanation. However, you should avoid certain symbols – they're listed below – and as for "up to a total of fourteen," some systems at least

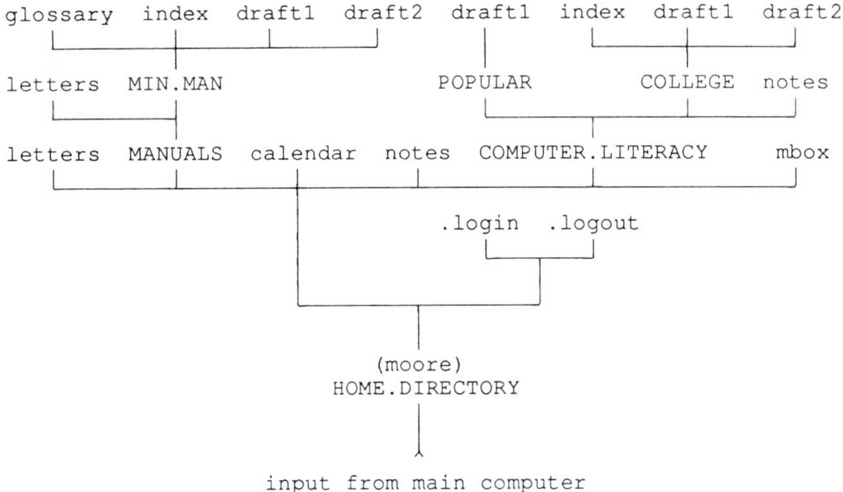

Figure 4.1: Diagram of Files and Directories

seem to tolerate file and directory names that are a lot longer. I've tried names up to 100 characters; then I got tired of trying. It's hard to type those real long names, though, so it's just as well to keep them at fourteen and under, just in case someone's looking over your shoulder and complains about it. File and directory names can't have any spaces in them, so if you want to separate words, use periods or underlines, for instance, "file.name" or "file_name." You can use symbols other than periods or underlines in file or directory names, but it isn't a good idea, because many symbols have a special meaning to the computer, and using them in a file or directory name can foul you up. If you insist on using symbols in your file names, **do not use** \, /, &, ?, <, >, |, [,], *, or ;. They'll just get you in trouble. *

---

* I don't give you a lot of hard and fast rules, so just humor me on this one. It can save you a lot of grief.

A good thing to do when you make directories is to capitalize their names. This is only a matter of convenience. You use different commands for getting into files than you use for directories; if you use a file command for a directory, or vice versa, the computer will tell you. But even so, capitalizing your directories will make them easier to spot.

I want to stress that you don't have to have different directories for different subjects, but if you don't, eventually things will get out of hand. It's incredibly easy to make multiple files, copies of a file, or to make small changes in a file when you use a computer, so files tend to proliferate like crazy. I know because I've been through it. Believe me, the hardest thing to get used to on a computer is housecleaning, identifying and pruning unwanted files, and putting inactive but desired files somewhere where they can be found.

My suggestions for avoiding this confusion are:

1. Capitalize directory names.

2. Make separate directories for different subjects, articles, talks, whatever.

3. Within each directory, make subdirectories (simply, a directory within a directory) for letters, notes, and old drafts and call them LETTERS, NOTES, and OLD.DRAFTS.

4. For files that are letters, use the name of the person or place the letter is being sent as the name of the file, possibly along with the date.

5. For files that are papers or articles, talks, etc., use as file names draft1, draft2, and so on. Leave only the latest draft in the main directory for that subject; put old drafts in the OLD.DRAFTS directory.

6. For files that are formatted (the Unix formatting system, called **roff**, is described in **Chapters 6** and **7**), use the file name followed by ".rf" for "roffed file," for example, draft2.rf.

Using these conventions has worked for me, but you can use other conventions if you like. As long as you are consistent, you'll be okay.

In the file diagram some of the files have a period in front of them. This means they are hidden files, ones you don't need to see very often (you use a special command option to see them – it's described in the section, **Listing Files and Directories**). You can make any file (or directory) hidden simply by putting a period in front of its name, but usually only special instructions to the computer are hidden. **Chapter 10 (Hidden Files)** explains what they are good for; please don't worry about them right now. You could use the computer for the rest of your life without ever knowing anything about them and do just fine. Some of them can make using the computer easier or more personal, though, so take a look at **Chapter 10** when the time comes.

The main computer contains files and directories, too. They contain the various programs you are using when you give the computer a command. You don't need to know *anything* about computer programs to *use* a computer. All you need to learn is how to make your files and directories, put stuff in them, take it out, change it, and put it back in. And that's what we'll learn in this chapter and the editing chapter that follows.

In this chapter we'll look at how to make files, write things in them, and look at existing files. Then you'll see how to remove files you don't want. Next will be how to list the files and directories you've made. After that I'll show you some handy commands for copying, moving, and finding files, and how to make and remove directories.

Making Files

There are two good ways to make a new file. The first, which works on any Unix system, uses the command **cat** (short for "concatenate." *Concatenate* means "to link together." The computer doesn't store a page full of text like a file cabinet. It breaks down the text into symbols representing each letter, number, *and* space. (There are no blanks in a computer mind.) When you want to pull something out of storage and look at it, the computer links together all the symbols and prints out your text. Hence the word *concatenate*. It's a real word. Go ahead, look it up.

The second method only works on the newer systems that have the **vi** (*visual*) editor. If you want to use the second method but don't know if your Unix system has the **vi** editor, just try the command as shown. If your system doesn't have **vi** editing, the computer will reply, ''Command not found.''

1. To make a file that you don't want to edit right away, tell the computer to print or link together (*concatenate*): % **cat** >*filename*[**RET**]

Then write anything here: *Type anything you like; as many lines as you like.* [**RET**]

When you're *done*, type on a separate line: **[CTRL]d**

Hold down the **CONTROL** key while you type **d**.

Now you have a file with whatever name you typed in up there where I wrote *filename*. Remember, file names can be a combination of letters, numbers, or symbols, but they cannot have any blank spaces in them.

2. If you want to edit your new file right away, type: % **vi** *filename* [**RET**]

This will create a file and put you into the **vi** editor mode, which allows you to make changes to files by changing letters, words, or lines – deleting or adding them, or moving things around. Those operations are described in detail in the next chapter. Right now I'll just tell you how to write (*append*) in the file you just made and how to save your text and leave the editor mode (*write* and *quit*).

To begin writing (*appending*) in your **vi**

editor file, type: **a**

Nothing visible will happen, but you will now be able to write.

To get back out of your new file, you *write* and *quit*: **[ESC]:wq[RET]**

This puts your file away and brings you back to the directory the file is in.

On some computer keyboards **[ESC]** (escape) is called **[ALT]** (alter).

Reading Files

To read an existing file when you don't want to change anything in it, you can do any of several things.

You can type: % **cat** *filename* **[RET]**

cat will keep printing the whole file on your screen without stopping, so it isn't too good for long files. If your terminal is hard-wire connected to the computer, the lines will whiz by so fast you probably won't be able to read them. There are two solutions to this: either stop and start the action on the screen with the **[CTRL]**s command or use the **more** command to stop after printing one screenful.

To *stop* the action on the screen: **[CTRL]s**

To restart after using **[CTRL]**s: **[SPACEBAR]**

To print one screenful at a time, type: % **more** *filename* **[RET]**

If you are using the **more** command and there is more than one screenful in the file, the computer will fill the screen, then stop and tell you what percentage of the file you've looked at so far, like this: more 40%

''More to see, 40% seen.''

If you want to see some more, you have a few choices. To see one more screenful, tap the space bar: **[SPACEBAR]**

If you want to see (*down*) another half screenful, type: **[CTRL]d**

Hold down the **[CTRL]** key while you type **d**.

If you want to see just one more line, type: **[RET]**

And if you want to *quit* looking at the file, type: **q[RET]**

The **head** and **tail** commands show you the first or last ten lines of a file. They are sometimes useful to help you remember what's in a file.

To print just the first ten lines of the file, type: % **head** *filename* **[RET]**

To print just the last ten lines of the file, type: % **tail** *filename* **[RET]**

If you want to able to jump back and forth in the file, you can use the command **view**, which is part of the **vi** editor and is explained in **Chapter 5**.

Removing Files

If you want to *remove* a file, type: % **rm** *filename* **[RET]**

This gets rid of your file for good, so be sure you really want to get rid of it. In **Chapter 10, Hidden Files**, there is a good command you can install that will ask you whether you really want to get rid of the file you are removing. You can then answer *yes* or *no* (**y** or **n**). This is a good safety feature, and it isn't hard to install.

Listing Files and Directories

To *list* all the (nonhidden) files and subdirectories in whatever directory you are in, type: % **ls[RET]**

If you want to *list all* the files and subdirectories in that directory, type: % **ls -a[RET]**

To list your files and directories in the order they were last changed, use "*list time*": % **ls -t[RET]**

To see your files and directories (with notes about their size in bytes and when they were last changed), type "*list long*": % **ls -l[RET]**

To *list* your files and directories with the file *sizes* listed in blocks: **% ls -s[RET]**

One **byte** equals one character, either a letter, number, or space. One *byte* is made up of eight **bits**, which are the basic units a computer understands. One **block** equals either 512, 1024, or 4096 *bytes*, depending on what system you are using. Your computer needs to know how many bytes your blocks contain. You don't.

Kilobytes are the unit of measure most often used in describing the capacity of a computer's memory, for instance, in ads proclaiming "IBM PC with 640K!" Because multiples of eight bits don't add up to an even thousand, one "kilobyte" actually equals 1024 bytes. *

There's an option you can use to list your files and directories with a symbol after them that tells you whether they are files or directories and whether the files are "executable," the way computer programs are. This can be handy. To *list* the *Form* of your files and directories: **% ls -F[RET]**

This option will list the ordinary file names with nothing after them and will place an asterisk after "executable" files and a slash after the directory names.

To list the files and directories contained in whatever directory you are in, *including* the contents of all the subdirectories, use this: **% ls -R[RET]**

---

* *I* know that "kilo" means 1000 (not 1024), and *you* know that "kilo" means 1000 (not 1024), so wouldn't you think *computer designers* would know? And some of them take *years* of math.

The **-R** actually means "recursive," a word that describes the action taken by the computer in going back and listing the contents of the subdirectories in a given directory after the files and subdirectory names in that directory have been listed. The word *recursive* doesn't tell you what the list will look like (unless you're a mathematician or computer programmer), so I use the word *roster*, since the command gives you a complete roster of directory and subdirectory contents.

The **ls** command uses the **cat** command to print the list on your screen, so if you have more than a few files and directories, the list will disappear from the top of the screen as fast as it appears at the bottom. This is especially true if you are using the **R** option. You can prevent this by telling the **ls** command to print using the **more** command. You do this by using a "pipe":

% **ls -R | more[RET]**

The **|** is the pipe. Now the list will fill the screen and stop until you give instructions to start again. Those instructions were shown earlier in this chapter.

The **|** is like the < and the > in that you can use spaces between the command and the symbol, or not, as you please, and the command will work just the same.

You can also combine these options. A good option to use with **R** is **C**, which prints out the list in multiple *Columns*: % **ls -RC | more[RET]**

You can combine others, too. Here are a couple of good combinations: % **ls -RCsa | more[RET]**

This lists all your files and directories, including hidden ones, and shows you their sizes in blocks.

This one will list all your files and directories, including hidden ones, show you their sizes in both bytes and blocks, and tell you when they were last changed: % **ls -Rsla | more[RET]**

You can do all of the above and have the files and directories you changed last listed first to make them easy to find: % **ls -Rslat | more[RET]**

Copying, Moving, and Finding Files

Next we have some fancier things you can do with your files.

To make a *copy* of a file: % **cp** *filename filename.cp* **[RET]**

If you're doing this just to have a copy of your file in case you mess it up, you should give the copy the same name as the original, followed with ".cp" or ".copy" (*filename.cp*) to remind you that it's a duplicate. You don't have to do this, but if you don't, sooner or later you will get confused. I know because I've done it.

Another good reason to make copies of files is for sucessive drafts. In this case, just number them, sucessively: % **cp draft1 draft2[RET]**

You then put away draft1 and start changing draft2.

To *move* or rename a file: % **mv** *oldfilename newfilename* **[RET]**

Here **mv**'s basic function is renaming a file. It can also do better tricks, like moving a file from one directory to another.

To *move* a file from the preceding directory into the one you're using, type: % **mv ..**/*filename filename***[RET]**

The two periods represent the directory just before the one you're in, no matter which directory that is.

To *move* a file from the directory you're using into a subdirectory, type: % **mv** *filename DIRECTORYNAME/filename***[RET]**

Be careful that your second file name isn't the same as one of your current files. If it is, **cp** or **mv** will write right over the top of it, *and your old file will be gone.* (See **Chapter 10** on hidden files for a command to make the computer double-check with you before writing over a file.)

You can add to an old file, though, without writing over it. To append one file to the end of another:

% **cat** *new.file* >> *old-.file* **[RET]**

For example:

% **cat** *index* >> *final-.draft* **[RET]**

To see how many words you have in a file, ask for a *word count* :

% **wc** *filename* **[RET]**

The computer will reply with numbers for:

lines | words | characters

If you can't remember which of your directories one of your files is in, you can use the command:

% **find . -name** *filename* **-print[RET]**

Here's an example using the set of files and directories diagrammed at the beginning of this chapter. If you are in your home directory and you type:

% **find . -name** *glossary* **-print[RET]**

The computer will print:

./MANUALS/MIN.MAN/-glossary

The slashes mark divisions between directories. The period represents the directory you are in.

If you've used the same file name in more than one directory, **find** will show you all the files with that name. Here's an example of that from the file diagram. If you type:

% **find . -name** *draft1* **-print[RET]**

The computer will print:

./COMPUTER.LITERACY/COLLEGE/draft1

./COMPUTER.LITERACY/POPULAR/draft1

./MANUALS/MIN.MAN/draft1

You can look at either of those draft1 files without changing directories by using either the **cat**, **more**, or **tail** commands described earlier and using the directory name(s) and slash marks, like this:

% **more MANUALS/MIN.MAN/draft1 [RET]**

Directories

To *make* a *directory*:

% **mkdir** *DIRECTORYNAME* **[RET]**

Like file names, directory names can be any combination of letters, numbers, or symbols but cannot contain any spaces.

To get into a directory (*change directory)*:

% **cd** *DIRECTORYNAME* **[RET]**

You can move over more than one directory at a time by using several directory names and using slash marks between them:

% **cd** *DIRECTORYNAME/DIRECTORYNAME* **[RET]**

Whenever you need to get back to your original home directory (from *any* directory), type: % **cd[RET]**

If you want to move to the directory just before the one you are in, type: % **cd ..[RET]**

And if you want to look at a file from the preceding directory you can use either the **cat**, **tail**, or **more** commands: % **cat** ../*filename* **[RET]**

If you want to put a *copy* of that file into the directory you are in: % **cp** ../*filename filename* **[RET]**

To *copy* a file from the directory you are in to a subdirectory, first, *make* the *directory* (**mkdir**) if it doesn't exist yet; then use the directory name followed by a slash and the desired file name: % **cp** *filename DIRECTORYNAME/filename* **[RET]**

When you're doing a lot of hopping around in your directory system you may occasionally need to see just where you are. To find out, ask for the "*path* of *working directory*": % **pwd[RET]**

The directory you are in is called your working directory. The computer will print the names of all the directories up to and including your working directory. If you were in the MIN.MAN directory in the file diagram and used the **pwd** command, the computer would print: /a/b/moore/MANUALS/MIN.MAN

Those directories in front of the account name ("moore") are part of the Unix system containing other accounts and commands.

To *remove* a *directory*: % **rmdir** *DIRECTORY-NAME* **[RET]**

This gets rid of a directory. But it won't work unless all the files in that directory have already been moved or gotten rid of.

Chapter 5

Editing

The vi (Visual) Editor

An editor can be used as you write your file or you can use it to edit the file later after someone else has typed it in. Some people like to make corrections on a printout and then use the editor to make those changes for the next printed draft. This saves a lot of typing time.

The best editing program to use on a Unix system is **vi**. They tried a couple of others in the days of real slow terminals and they were not nearly as easy to use. The **vi** stands for "visual": You can see the changes happen as you make them. Unlike the earlier programs used on Unix, it shows you when you make an editing mistake. If you never made mistakes, you'd never need an editing program. If you're not sure whether or not your system has **vi**, try making a file by typing **vi** *filename* **[RET]**. If it makes a file, you've got it. If it says "command not found," you don't have it, and you'll have to use the **ed** editor described at the back end of this chapter. Every Unix system has **ed**.

You can either make a new file and edit it as you go, or duplicate one of your present files, edit it, and put the edited version back in the file you took it from. If you want to keep both an old and a new draft, you should make a copy of the file first, then edit the copy to make your new draft.

So, first, make a *copy* of your file:	% **cp** *filename filename2* **[RET]**

If you do this, it's a good idea to give both files the same name, with a "2" at the end of the new version. This makes it easier to remember that they are different versions of the same file and tells you which one is the more recent version.

To put a copy of one of your existing files in the editor so that you can edit it (or to make a new file), type:

% **vi** *filename* **[RET]**

This puts you in the editor. While you're in the editor, you won't see the prompt ($ or %) before your commands. There are two modes within the **vi** editor: **append mode** (for adding text) and editor **command mode** (for giving commands to move around or to delete or put in lines). You can get into append mode by pushing **a** (or the commands **A**, **i**, **I**, **o**, **O**, **c**, and **C**, described later in this chapter) and into editor command by pushing **[ESC]** (escape). As mentioned earlier, on some terminal keyboards **[ESC]** may be called **[ALT]** (alter).

When you want to write *(append)*, type:

a

Nothing will change on the screen, but you will now be able to write.

When you want to give a command to the editor, you *escape* from append mode:

[ESC]

Nothing will change on the screen until you give the command.

Editing commands are coming up in a few pages.

When you want to put the edited file away and return to the directory it is stored in, just *write* and *quit*: **[ESC]:wq[RET]**

Any commands you give to the computer editor that begin with a colon will appear at the bottom of the screen, like this: :wq

Every so often as you are editing, you should use the *write* command to save any changes you've made: **[ESC]:w[RET]**

This will prevent a lot of anguish if someone trips over the cord and pulls the plug on your terminal. If the terminal gets disconnected somehow before you've used *write*, any additions or changes you've made since the last time you used *write* will be gone.

If you have given a command or two and can't remember whether you are in append or editor command mode, don't worry. If you push **a** when you are in append mode, it will just type "a" and you can erase that easily. If you are in editor command mode and you push **[ESC]**, you will hear a beep, but nothing bad will happen. So when you are not sure, don't be afraid to push the **[ESC]** key.

Coming up is a list of commands you can give to the **vi** editor. Some move the cursor, the little box or blinking line of light that marks your place on the screen as you type. Some allow you to insert or change letters or words or to delete lines and put them somewhere else or get rid of them. Go slow at first and you'll find that editing is pretty easy. It's also fun to watch the text change right in front of you, without erasures and crossing out. **The one command to remember always is the u command**. It stands for *"undo,"* and it reverses the last command you made. So even if you goof, you can fix it.

Now I'll run through the **vi** editor commands and show you how they are typed out and what they mean. We'll start with the simpler commands; later I'll show you the more advanced commands. You can get along fine with only a few commands, and when you get comfortable with those, you can use the more advanced commands to make editing even easier. You don't have to memorize all the commands; that's what the lists of commands in this book are for. Just prop up the book so that you can see it while you're editing.

First, I'll cover how to make changes to letters and words. *Second,* I'll show how to move the cursor around. The *third* section following shows deleting part or all of a line or lines. The *fourth* is probably the most fun: moving lines from one place to another.

vi Editing

To enter the writing mode and *append* one or more letters or spaces just after the cursor: **a**

To *escape* from append (writing) mode to the command mode: **[ESC]**

To *undo* the last command: **u**

To *insert* one or more letters or spaces just in front of the cursor: **i**

To *replace* a letter you're on: **r**

To erase a letter or space: **x**

To *change* a *word*, placing the cursor on the first letter: **cw**

To change a letter from upper- to lower-case, or vice versa: **~**

To *change* a line, from where you are to the end of the line: **C**

To move up, or *climb* (*"klimb"*), one line: **k**

or use a directional arrow: **↑**

To move down or *jump*, one line: **j**

or use a directional arrow: **↓**

To move forward one space: **l**

or tap:	**[SPACEBAR]**
or use a directional arrow:	→
To move back one space:	**h**
or tap:	**[BACKSPACE]**
or use a directional arrow:	←
To go to the *beginning* of the next *Word*:	**W**
To go the *End* of the next *word*:	**E**
To go *Back* to the *Beginning* of the previous *word*:	**B**
To go to the *beginning* of the next *"word"* (treats punctuation as a word):	**w**
To go to the *end* of the next *"word"* (treats punctuation as a word):	**e**
To go *back* to the *beginning* of the previous *"word"* (treats punctuation as a word):	**b**
To *Go* to the last line of the file:	**G**
To *Go* to the *first* line of the file:	**1G**
To *Go* to a specified line in the file:	*specified number* **G**
Or you can go to a specified line by:	**:***specified number* **[RET]**

You don't have to set visible line numbers to use these commands to go to a specified line number, but if you want to *set* visible line *numbers*: **:set nu[RET]**

This sets visible line numbers for the whole file but doesn't run the whole file past you to do it.

To get *no numbers*, you unset the line numbers: **:set nonu[RET]**

Set wrapmargin is a good command to use: **:set wm=***number***[RET]**

It's like having a typewriter with an automatic carriage return. **:set wm=** makes the computer automatically start a new line as if you had hit **[RET]** when you get to a designated number of spaces from the right edge of the screen. If you're in the middle of a word it puts the whole word on the next line instead of splitting it. So setting **:set wm=10** will make the computer hit the return key when you get ten spaces from the right margin.

When you are editing and use a command that starts with a colon (:), the command will appear at the bottom of the screen. Other **vi** commands will be invisible.

Note: Using numbers in front of commands will make your editing faster.

Notice the use of numbers when moving the cursor, that little box or blinking line that marks your position. You can put a number in front of any command involving movement. Then the cursor will move that number of letters or lines in the direction you tell it. When you get used to this, editing will be faster, but until you do, hitting the command key to repeat movement will work just fine.

Putting a number in front of the command like this works for most of the editor commands. For instance, **23G** = Go to line 23; **3cW** = change 3 Words; **4j** = jump down 4 lines; etc. It is especially handy for deleting and moving lines, our next topic.

vi Editing: Deleting and Duplicating

When you use a *delete* command in the **vi** editor, the letter, word or words, or line or lines disappear. The *last* item you deleted can be gotten back later by using *put* (see below). This is how you move things from one spot to another. *Yank* is similar, except that the yanked lines are duplicated and do not disappear from their original location.

To *delete* to the end of a *Word*:	**dW**
To *delete* to the end of a "*word*":	**dw**
When you use the lowercase *w*, the editor treats punctuation as "words."	
To *Delete* from your position to the end of a line:	**D**
To *delete* a whole line:	**dd**
To *delete* a specified number of lines:	*specified number* **dd**
To duplicate a specified number of lines to be put elsewhere, use *yank*:	*specified number* **yy**

vi Editing: Moving

To copy a line or lines or move them to a different place, first *yank* the line or lines (to *copy* them) or *delete* them (to *move* them). Move the cursor where you want the lines to be. Then *put* them below the cursor: **p**

Or *Put* them above the cursor: **P**

Either of these commands will open up enough lines to put the new lines in without erasing any existing lines, even if there is no space between lines at present.

vi Editing: Advanced Deleting, Duplicating, and Moving

The *put* commands above will only retrieve the last item deleted or yanked. If you want to retrieve something you deleted or yanked earlier, you can do it with this version of *put*. Deleted or yanked lines go into temporary buffers (storage areas) that are labeled with numbers. The contents of those buffers can be retrieved like this: "*number* **p**

or: "*number* **P**

"**1p** retrieves the last deleted or yanked item, "**2p** the next to last, and so on.

If you expect to use the item you are deleting or yanking at a later time but will probably be deleting or yanking a number of lines between now and then, you can label the deleted or yanked items with letters: "*letter* **dd**

or: "*letter* **yy**

This can work for any type of deleting or yanking you are doing, whether it's one letter or a hundred lines.

"q4dd, for example, will delete four lines and put them in a labeled buffer whose contents you can retreive with **"qp** or **"qP**, like this: "*letter* **p**

or: "*letter* **P**

However, when you leave the editor, the contents of all the buffers, whether labeled with numbers or letters, will disappear.

vi Editing: Advanced Commands

These are some of the more advanced commands you can give.

To *Append* at the *end* of the line you are in: **A**

To *Insert* at the *beginning* of the line you are in: **I**

To *Join* the next line to the end of this one: **J**

To move forward one line: **+**

To move to the *start* of the *previous* line: **-**

To move to the *start* of the *next* line: **[RET]**

To move to the *start* of *this* line: **0**

To move to the *end* of *this* line: **$**

To move to the first *(Home)* line on the screen: **H**

To move to the *Last* line on the screen:	**L**
To move to the *Middle* line on the screen:	**M**
To *open* up a space *below* the cursor and begin writing on the new line:	**o**
To *Open* up a space *above* the cursor and begin writing on the new line:	**O**
To search forward for a word or pattern (may be part of a word):	/*word or pattern* **[RET]**
To search backward for a word or pattern:	?*word or pattern* **[RET]**
You use **n** or **N** to search for the *next* appearance of that word or pattern.	
To continue a search in the initial direction:	**n**
To search in the opposite direction from the original search:	**N**
If you want to search for both "woman" and "women," you can replace the odd letter with a period:	/*wom.n* **[RET]**
Or to search for "man" and "men" *and* "woman" and "women":	/*m.n* **[RET]**

This will also find words like "*man*uscript" and "re*min*der," because they contain an *m* and an *n* separated by another letter.

The search commands using / and **?** can also be used after a colon (:/*word*), but the follow-up **n** or **N** will work just the opposite of the way described above: The **n** reverses the direction of search, and the **N** continues the search in the initial direction. Why didn't they make both follow-ups the same when the initial commands are so similar? There is no good reason. I only mention it so you can figure out what's going on if the computer seems to be acting up on you while you are searching with the **vi** editor.

You can also use these to keep from getting confused about the direction you are searching in. The first *always* repeats a search in a forward direction: //

And this one *always* repeats by going backwards: **??**

Table I: List of Commands for the vi Editor

To escape from append (writing) mode to command mode:	**[ESC]**
[ESC] = Escape. This may be labeled **[ALT]** for *alter*, on some terminals.	
To *undo* last change:	**u**
To *append* (write):	**a**
To *Append* at the end of this line:	**A**
To *insert* characters (characters can be either letters, numbers, spaces, or whatever special characters your keyboard types, such as mathematical symbols) just before cursor:	**i**
To *Insert* characters at the beginning of this line:	**I**
To change the case of this letter from upper- to lowercase, or vice versa:	**~**
To erase a letter or space and close up the space between words:	**x**
To erase a specified number of characters (letters, numbers, *and* spaces):	*number of characters* **x**
To *replace* (change) a character:	**r**

Remember, you can put numbers in front of most of these commands to replace more than one letter, change more than one word, move more than one word or line, etc.

To *change* a *word* (you must be on the first letter of the word):	**cw**
To *Change* the rest of the line:	**C**
To *Join* the next line to the end of this line:	**J**
To *set* line *numbers*:	**:set nu[RET]**
To unset line numbers (*(set no umbers)*:	**:set no nu[RET]**
To *set wrapmargin* (automatic return):	**:set wm=***number* **[RET]**
To go to line number specified:	**:***line number* **[RET]**
This works even without visible line numbers.	
To *Go* to line number specified:	*line number* **G**
To *Go* to end of file:	**G**
To *Go* to beginning of file:	**1G**
Before each command, *escape* from append mode to command mode:	**[ESC]**
To move to the *beginning* of next *Word*:	**W**
To move to the *End* of next word:	**E**
To move to the *Beginning* of previous word:	**B**
To move to the *beginning* of next "*word*" (treats punctuation as a word):	**w**

To move to the *end* of the next *"word"* (treats punctuation as a word):	**e**
To move to the *beginning* of the previous *"word"* (treats punctuation as a word):	**b**
To move back one space:	**h**
or use a directional arrow:	←
To move forward one space:	**l**
or tap:	**[SPACEBAR]**
or use a directional arrow:	→
To move down *(jump)* one line:	**j**
or use a directional arrow:	↓
To move up *(climb)* one line:	**k**
or use a directional arrow:	↑
To move to the *start* of *this* line:	**0**
To move to the *end* of *this* line:	**$**
To move to the *start* of the *next* line:	**[RET]**
To move to the *start* of the *previous* line:	**-**
To move *forward* (down) one line:	**+**
To move *forward* a specified number of lines:	*number of lines* **+**

To move to the first, or *Home*, line on the screen:	**H**
To move to the *Last* line on the screen:	**L**
To move to the *Middle* line on the screen:	**M**
To *delete* the line you are on:	**dd**
To *delete* a specified number of lines:	*number of lines* **dd**
To *Delete* to the end of the line:	**D**
To *delete* to the end of the *Word* you are in:	**dW**
To *delete* to the end of the *"word"* you are in (treats punctuation as a word):	**dw**
To duplicate *(yank)* the line you are on:	**yy**
To duplicate *(yank)* a specified number of lines:	*number of lines* **yy**
To *put* deleted lines just below cursor:	**p**
To *Put* deleted lines just above cursor:	**P**
To *open* a line below the cursor (puts you in append mode):	**o**
To *Open* a line above the cursor (puts you in append mode):	**O**
To scroll the file forward *(down)* a few lines:	**[CTRL]d**

To scroll the file *forward* more and redraw the screen:	**[CTRL]f**
To scroll the file back *(up)* a few lines:	**[CTRL]u**
To scroll the file *back* more and redraw the screen:	**[CTRL]b**
To *write* and *quit* (puts the edited file back into its original file and takes you out of the editing mode):	**:wq[RET]**

A Few More Handy Commands for the vi Editor

These commands are borrowed from the **ed** editor system. Although the **ed** editor is not as good a system as **vi**, it does have a few handy commands that make it attractive. However, the good **ed** commands can be used on the **vi** system by using **[ESC]:** in front of them. These commands appear in the section on the **ed** editor, but since they can be helpful while you're using the **vi** editor, I've included them here, too.

Before each command:	**[ESC]**
To *substitute* a word or words:	**:s/***old word***/***new word***/[RET]**
To *substitute* each time the word or words appear(s) on that line, add the **g** *(global)* command:	**:s/***old word***/***new word***/g[RET]**
To *substitute* the word(s) on several lines, say, 1 through 6:	**:1,6s/***old word***/***new word***/g[RET]**

If you want to *substitute* everywhere the

word or words appear(s) in the file, type:	**:1,$s/***old word***/***new word***/g[RET]**
This is handy to correct misspelling throughout the file.	
To get rid of a word, you can *substitute* "nothing" for it:	**:s/***old word***//[RET]**
To *add* word(s) behind a word or phrase, use **&**:	**:s/***old word***/&** *added words***/[RET]**
The **&** tells the computer to print the old word(s) in front of the added words instead of substituting.	
To *move* a line from one place to another:	**:***line number to be moved***m***line number for it to be placed after***[RET]**
To *move* several lines to the end of the file, type:	**:***line number,line number***m$[RET]**
To *move* the line you are on:	**:m***line number for it to be placed after* **[RET]**
To find out what line you're on when you aren't using visible line numbers:	**.=[RET]**
To place *(read)* the contents of a specified filename on the line(s) after the line number, say, line 860:	**:860r** *specified filename* **[RET]**

To *write* a copy of lines 860 through 960 from the file you are editing in a different file for later use: **:860,960w** *filename* **[RET]**

To *write* a copy of line 860 through the end of the file into a new file, for instance, as an index: **:860,$w** *index* **[RET]**

$ signifies the last line in the file.

The ed Editor

An editor can be used either to write your file or to edit it later after someone else has typed it in. Some people like to make corrections on a printout and then use the editor to make those changes for the next printed draft. This saves a lot of typing time.

The **ed** editor is an earlier and decidedly more primitive editing system than the **vi** editor. Unfortunately, some Unix systems don't come with the **vi** editor; the later Unix systems give you a choice. If you have a choice, use **vi**. If you are not sure whether or not you have **vi**, just try making a file by typing **vi** *filename* **[RET]**. If it makes a file, you've got it. If it says "command not found," you don't have it. Too bad. Just about every Unix system has the **ed** editor, though.

When you use the **ed** editor, all your commands show up on the screen, down at the bottom. The changes you make with those commands don't show up at all unless you insist, by using the *print* command, which is explained in the next section. Unless you're awfully sure of your editing changes, it's a good idea to include the *print* command with each of those editing commands so that you can make sure you've accomplished what you wanted to do. Well, let's jump right in.

To pull one of your files for editing, or to create a new file, type:	% **ed** *filename* **[RET]**
To write *(append)* in the file, use:	**a**
Like the **vi** editor, the **ed** editor doesn't give you a prompt, such as %, $, or #. If you give a wrong command or tell it to open a file that doesn't exist yet, **ed** will give you one of these:	?
This means **ed** doesn't know what's going on — just give another command. You don't have to explain yourself to a computer.	
To get out of the append (writing) mode into the command mode, use a period on	

a line by itself, like this:	**.[RET]**
To put the changed file away and return to the directory it is filed in, *write*:	**w[RET]**
and *quit*:	**q[RET]**
When you put your **ed** edited file away that way, it will write over the previous draft. If you want to keep both old and new drafts, use the *write* command with a new file name:	**w** *filename2* **[RET]**
then:	**q[RET]**
If you messed up the edited version and don't want to save it, just *quit*:	**q[RET]**
Ed will ask you if you really mean to do this by saying:	?
If you really don't want to save the file, just type **q** again:	**q[RET]**
If you want to save the file but goofed, either type **w** for *write* and then *quit*, or give another editing command if you want to keep editing.	
To reverse *(undo)* the last command you gave the editor:	**u**

To See Your ed Editing

When you use the **ed** editor to edit an existing file, you may be dismayed when you tell **ed** to get your file for you. All that shows up on the screen is the number of characters you have written there. Don't worry, this is what **ed** considers normal. You have to ask it to print the lines you want to see. Maybe some folks can edit blindfolded, but I like to see what I'm doing, so let's look at how to print out some lines. First, pull out a file using the **ed** *filename* **[RET]** command.

To *print* a specified line: *line number* **p[RET]**

To *print* a range of lines, for instance 4 through 10: **4,10p[RET]**

To *print* all the lines in the file: **1,$p[RET]**

$ signifies the last line in the file, so you can use this command to print from any line in the file to the end of that file.

ed Editing

To write at the end of the file, use *append*:

a[RET]
your words here — as many lines as you like **[RET]**
.[RET]

The period placed on a line by itself is the instruction to the editor to implement the command. Some of the **ed** editor commands get an immediate response from **ed** when you push **[RET]**. If you don't get a response after you give a command and push **[RET]**, you need to type a period on a line by itself and follow it with **[RET]**.

To write at the beginning of the file, use *insert*:

i[RET]
your words here — as many lines as you like **[RET]**
.[RET]

To *append* after a specified line:	*line number* **a[RET]** *your words here — as many lines as you like* **[RET]** **.[RET]**
To *insert* before a specified line:	*line number* **i[RET]** *your words here — as many lines as you like* **[RET]** **.[RET]**
To find out what line you are on:	**.=**
To move forward one line and print it, just hit:	**[RET]**
To move back one line and print it, type:	**-[RET]**
To *print* a specified number of lines before the line you are on:	**.-***number of lines* **,.p[RET]**
To *print* a specified number of lines after the line you are on:	**.,.+***number of lines* **p[RET]**
This can be also used to *print* several lines before *and* after the one you are on:	**.-***no. of lines***,.+***no. of lines* **p[RET]**
To change a word or words, you use **s** *(substitute)*. It looks like this:	**s** */old word/new word/***[RET]**
It will look as though nothing has happened until you type *print*:	**p[RET]**

But even if you don't print it, the change will have been made. This is the danger of the **ed** editor.

Also, this only substitutes the word(s) in the line you are on (remember, use **.=** to find out what line you are on), and it only does it the first time the word appears in that line. If you want all occurrences of the word(s) in that line substituted, add the **g** *(global)* command:

s/*old word*/*new word*/**g[RET]**

Or if you want the word(s) *substituted* on several lines, say, 1 through 6, type:

1,6s/*old word*/*new word*/**g[RET]**

If you want to *substitute* the word(s) everywhere they appear in the file, type:

1,$s/*old word*/*new word*/**g[RET]**

This is handy for correcting spelling mistakes.

You can get rid of a word or phrase this way, by *substituting* "nothing" for it:

s/*old word*//**[RET]**

To add word(s) behind a word or phrase, use **&**:

s/*old word*/**&***added words*/**[RET]**

The **&** tells the computer to print the old word(s) in front of the added word(s) instead of substituting.

To *change* a whole line:

line number **c[RET]**
type the new line or lines here **[RET]**
.[RET]

You can *change* several lines by using a comma between the lines:

line number, line number **c[RET]**
type the new line or lines here **[RET]**
.[RET]

To *delete* a line, type:

line number **d[RET]**

To *delete* from one line number up through another line number, type:

line number, line number **d[RET]**

Be careful with *delete*. When you are working with the **vi** editor, you can get back deleted lines, but when you are working with the **ed** editor, deleted lines are gone forever.

When you want to *move* lines from one place to another, you use the **m** command:

line number to be moved **m** *line number to be placed after* **[RET]**

To *move* several lines to the end of the file, type:

line number, line number **m$[RET]**

To *move* the line you are on (remember, you can use **.=** to find out what line you are on):

m*line number to be placed after* **[RET]**

If you want to place *(write)* copies of say, lines 21 through 42 from the file you are editing into a new file for later use:

21,42w *filename* **[RET]**

To search forward for a word or phrase, type: */word or phrase/*[**RET**]

If you want to repeat the search for the same word or phrase, type: //[**RET**]

And continue once again by repeating: //[**RET**]

If the word or phrase only shows up once in the file, the **ed** editor will find and print the same sentence as many times as you type //[**RET**].

For example, if you want to search for any instances of both the words "chimp" and "chimpanzee," you could just use */chimp/*, because "chimp" is part of "chimpanzee." But if you want to search for both "woman" and "women," you can replace the odd letter with a period: */wom.n/*[**RET**]

To search backward for a word or phrase, type: **?***word or phrase* **?**[**RET**]

And you can repeat the search with: **??**[**RET**]

Table II: List of Commands for the ed Editor

To pull one of your files for editing, or to create a new file:	% **ed** *filename* **[RET]**
After each command:	**[RET]**
To write *(append)* at the end of the file:	**a** *your words here* .
To write at the beginning of the file *(insert)*:	**i** *your words here* .
To *append* after a specified line:	*line number* **a** *your words here* .
To *insert* before a specified line:	*line number* **i** *your words here* .
To get out of the append mode into the command mode:	.
To reverse *(undo)* the last command that you gave the editor:	**u**
To *print* a specified line:	*line number* **p**
To *print* a range of lines, for example, 4 through 10:	**4,10p**
To *print* all the lines in the file:	**1,$p**
To *print* the line you are on:	**p**

To find out what line you are on:	**.=**
To move forward one line and print it:	**[RET]**
To move back one line and print it:	**-[RET]**
To *print* a line several lines before the line you are on:	**.-***number of lines* **p**
To *print* a line several lines after the line you are on:	**.+***number of lines* **p**
To *substitute* a word or words:	**s/***old word***/***new word***/**
To *substitute* each time the word or words appear(s) on that line, add the **g** *(global)* command:	**s/***old word***/***new word***/g**
To *substitute* the word(s) on several lines, say, 1 through 6:	**1,6s/***old word***/***new word***/g**
If you want to *substitute* everywhere the word or words appear(s) in the file:	**1,$s/***old word***/***new word***/g**
To get rid of a word:	**s/***old word***//**
To add word(s) behind a word or phrase, use **&**:	**s/***old word***/&***added words***/**
To *change* a whole line:	*line number* **c** *type the new line or lines here* **.**
To *change* several lines:	*line number,line number* **c** *type the new line or lines here* **.**

To *delete* a line:	*line number* **d**
To *delete* several lines:	*line number,line number* **d**
To *move* a line from one place to another:	*line number to be moved* **m** *line number to be placed after*
To *move* several lines to the end of the file:	*line number, line number* **m$**
To *move* the line you are on:	**m***line number to be placed after*
To place *(write)* copies of, say, lines 21 through 42 from the file you are editing into a new file for later use:	**21,42w** *filename*
To search forward for a word or phrase:	*/word or phrase/*
To repeat the search for the same word or phrase:	//
To repeat the search again:	//
If you want to search for both "woman" and "women":	*/wom.n/*
To look backward for a word or phrase:	**?***word or phrase* **?**
To repeat a backwards search:	**??**
To put the file away and return to the directory it is filed in, *write*:	**w**
and *quit*:	**q**

If you want to keep both old and new drafts, use the *write* command with a new file name:	**w** *filename2*
then *quit*:	**q**
If you messed up the edited version and don't want to save it, just *quit* without *writing*:	**q**

Chapter 6

Formatting for an Attractive Printout

Unix system formatting is a potent if primitive system. The problem is that it's a two-part system. You type commands, called "macros," before your text and interspersed within it (as described in this chapter), but you don't see the results of your commands until you *run off* the text, using one of the Unix system's **roff** commands (described in the next chapter, **Formatting and Printing**). The good part of Unix formatting is that all you (okay, I mean *us*) punk typists can make a good-looking page without spending ten years learning how to type like a pro.

A Note to Pro Typists

For you pros out there – well, you can type on the computer just as you'd type on a typewriter and never use a formatter (although thanks to computer and computer printer designers, you probably won't be able to underline anything). But using formatting macros makes changing page or paragraph layout much easier. Especially if *anything* you type will *ever* be typeset (and you can typeset on a laser printer nowadays), formatting macros are a must, because each typeset letter is a particular width, and trying to make columns or margins line up will be well nigh impossible without letting the computer do it for you.

The Unix formatting programs can take care of those spacing problems. You can also vary line length, set page offset, automatically put dates, page numbers, or titles at either the top or the bottom of the page, or easily make the whole thing double spaced for draft printouts and single spaced for a final printout. To change these specifications, you only need to change a few formatting macros. No extensive editing or retyping. Of course, maybe the people you type for never ask for the improbable. Believe me, using formatting macros will help a lot.

Using Macros

Macros are actually very simple computer programs that make several things happen by giving only one command. You can make your own macros if you like, but there are several macro packages with a lot of useful macro commands already set up, so you don't need to develop your own unless you want to. Most people never find it necessary to make any of their own macros.

Formatting macros are placed in the text, each on a line by itself. They show up just like regular text while you type and edit, but they disappear after you put the text through the formatting program. Only their effects remain.

You will see that each macro begins with a period and consists of several letters, numbers, or symbols. The letters in the **-mm** and **-ms** macro packages are capitalized; the standard **nroff/troff** macros and the **-me** macros are lowercase. Be sure to type the macros you use correctly, otherwise they will be ignored as commands, and if you forget to type the period at the beginning of the macro, the macro will be printed with the rest of your typing as regular text. If you follow the way the macros are typed in this chapter, you will not run into this problem.

At first, it will probably be easier to type in most of the macros after you have done your initial writing. You might want to start putting in the paragraph macros and the underline macros as your first "format as you go" tactic. If you learn to put in all of your macro commands as you type, you will be ready for printout sooner. But it will work just the same if you put them in later.

nroff, troff, and Macro Packages

There are two basic **roff** (''run off'') programs: **nroff** and **troff**. They are supposed to be pronounced ''**en**-roff'' and ''**tee**-roff,'' but I say them the way I see them, just to be cantankerous, I guess. **nroff** is used to get your text ready for a printer, and **troff** is used to get your text ready for a phototypesetter. Most folks don't have access to a phototypesetter, but many of the new laser printers can use **troff** typesetting commands. When **troff** is being used on some typesetters and most laser printers, it's called **ditroff**, for ''**d**evice-**i**ndependent **troff**.'' In any event, most of the commands do exactly the same thing on either **nroff** or **troff**. The exceptions occur when a typesetter can do something that a printer can't, such as change type size or style. For instance, in **troff**, the **-ms** command **.I** makes the next line italics; you can't do that with most printers, so in **nroff**, the **.I** command underlines each character in the next line. I'll note these exceptions as I explain the commands.

Now to the different macro packages available. The standard one doesn't have any name. The computer uses it whenever you tell it to **nroff** or **troff** your text, unless you add the name of one of the other macro packages as an *option*. This is done by typing a dash followed by the option. I show this in the chapter on printing, which follows this one. The best results will be gotten by combining macros from the Standard Macros and any *one* of the optional macro packages. If there is a macro in the optional package you're using that does the same thing as a macro from the standard macros, use the one from the optional package. It will be more likely to be compatible with the other macros you are using. (An example is setting line length when using the **-ms** macros. Instead of using the standard line length macro, **.ll**, use the **-ms** macro **.nr LL.**) Macros from the optional macro packages should not be mixed. The program won't work properly if you mix them.

The macro packages most common on Unix systems are **-ms** and **-mm**. The University of California has developed the **-me** macro package, found on many systems that feature the ''Berkeley enhancements.'' It's a very nice package and has some good features (such as automatic footnote numbering) that have been incorporated into revised **-ms** packages.

How to Start

You should start using formatting macros the same way you start using editing commands: be selective. Tyro typists will be likely to find more macros useful at first than the pros will. Look over the section and see what the macros do. If one of them sounds useful, try using it. All the macros can be useful, but this may not be evident at first. Adding macros to your repertoire a few at a time is the best way to learn. If you reckon you can type something as easily as you can put in a macro, don't complain about it, just don't use the macro. You won't hurt your computer's feelings.

How many formatting macros are useful to you will depend a lot on your skill as a typist. The most useful and often necessary ones to use in each package are the ones that set the page offset (right-side margin), line length (which will determine the left-side margin), and header and footer margins (to set the amount of space at the top and bottom of the page). Also look at underlining and dates (this is important, because using the **-ms** macro formatting program on your text will print a date on each page unless you tell it not to). The first section in this chapter lists the commands used with the standard macro package; second are the **-ms** macro commands; third, I list the **-mm** macros; and last are the **-me** macros.

What If I Don't Use Macros?

If you format your text using **nroff** and you don't use any macros, here's what you'll get: No **page offset** (no left-side margin). **Line length** will be 6.5 inches and lines will be **single spaced**. The text will be **filled** (a short line will have words from the next line added to it to fill in the line until it reaches the 6.5-inch line length), unless the next line is blank or if it begins with a blank, as in the case of an indented paragraph. **nroff** will also **hyphenate** words (using its internal dictionary) to help the line reach 6.5 inches; then it will **adjust** the line by leaving small amounts of extra space here and there so that both sides of the text line up evenly.

By using a few macros you can easily specify your **page offset**, set a different **line length**, request **double or triple spacing** instead of **single spacing**, or tell the computer you want **no fill, no hyphenation**, or **no adjustment** of your text.

The Standard nroff/troff Macro Commands

Macro commands that set spaces or distances, such as page offset, line or page length, or indentation, should be followed by a number and one of the units of measure described below. If you don't use a unit of measure after the number the measurement will be in number of **m**'s (ems) for horizontal space and number of vertical (line) spaces for vertical space (at least that's logical). For most folks, vertical space measured in **v**'s (''vertical spaces'') or paragraph indentation measured in ems (which are approximately the width of the letter *m*) are easier to visualize than, for instance, line lengths in ems. To get predictable results in horizontal measurements you can use your choice of measurement unit shown below. Simply use whatever units you are most familiar and comfortable with.

Any vertical distance you want to set (such as **.sp**, or *leave space*) can use *any* of these units of measure; any horizontal distance (such as **.po**, or *page offset*) can be set with any units *except* for the vertical line space unit, **v**.

i = inches

c = centimeters

m = ems: a somewhat arbitrary measurement invented by typesetters; on a typesetter with **troff** it's approximately the width of the letter **m**; in **nroff** it's equal to one space.

n = ens: on a typesetter with **troff** it's half the width of an **m**; in **nroff** it's the same width as an **m**.

P = a pica (1/6 inch)

p = a point (1/72 inch)

v = a vertical line space

u = a ''basic unit,'' a typesetting measurement that is 1/432 inch in **troff** and 1/240 inch in **nroff**.

page **o**ffset:	**.po** *number*
Sets the left-hand margin.	
The default value in **nroff**:	0 inches
The default value in **troff**:	26/27 inches

line length:	**.ll** *number*
Together with the page offset, this sets the right-hand margin.	
The default value in **nroff** and **troff**:	6.5 inches
single space:	**.ls 1**
Only needed if you are going back to single spacing after using double or other spacing.	
double space, triple space, etc.:	**.ls** *number*
page length:	**.pl** *number*
The default value in **nroff** and **troff**:	11 inches
begin new page:	**.bp**
During printing, this moves the paper the proper amount to start a new page.	
begin new page and number it:	**.bp** *number*
Following pages will be numbered incrementally and automatically.	
page number of next page equals (number):	**.pn** *number*
Following pages will be numbered automatically. This can be placed on any line of the preceding page.	
fill in:	**.fi**
Adds words from following lines to make up specified line length.	
no fill:	**.nf**
Leaves the lines as they are typed.	

break to a new line: **.br**

Does not *fill* the preceding line.

no adjust: **.na**

Fills words but doesn't add spaces; leaves the right margin uneven.

adjust **b**oth: **.ad b**

Makes both margins even.

When changing from one style of adjusting to another, put some sort of macro, such as **.br** or **.sp 0**, between the last line of text and the **.ad** macro. If you don't, the last line of text *before* the **.ad** macro will be adjusted in the new style.

adjust **l**eft: **.ad l**

Leaves right margin uneven.

adjust **r**ight: **.ad r**

Leaves left margin uneven.

adjust **c**enter: **.ad c**

Centers all lines – leaves both margins uneven.

center: **.ce**

Centers next line only.

center the next *number* of lines: **.ce** *number*

Centers several lines.

indent: **.in** *number*

Indents all following lines a given *number* of spaces.

temporary **i**ndent: **.ti** *number*

Indents the next line a given *number* of

spaces (or another unit of measure, if used).

leave one **sp**ace: **.sp**

Leaves one space between lines. If you need to leave space on a new page before any text appears, you need to use **.sv**.

leave **sp**ace(s): **.sp** *number*

Leaves space(s) between lines.

sa**v**e space: **.sv** *number*

Leaves blank space between or before lines; good for leaving space for figures or photos.

need space: **.ne** *number*

This is used to keep a group of lines (or a table) together. It prints the next *number* of lines unless there isn't room for all of them, in which case it saves them and prints them as soon as there is room.

italicize (in **troff**) or
under**l**ine (in **nroff**): **.ul**

Underlines only letters and numbers, not punctuation or spaces.

italicize (in **troff**) or
continuous **u**nderline (in **nroff**): **.cu**

Underlines letters, numbers, punctuation, *and* spaces.

no **h**yphenation: **.nh**

Turns off automatic hyphenation. If *you* hyphenated any words, they will be left alone.

hyphenate: **.hy 1**

Turns automatic hyphenation back on.

hyphenate: **.hy 14**

Automatic hyphenation is on, but the first two or last two letters in a word will not be split off by themselves.

hyphenate **w**ord(s): **.hw** *first-word second-word third-word etc.*

You can specify where you want words hyphenated, too. Just hyphenate the word or words the way you want them to be hyphenated if the necessity to do so arises. Separate each word with a space.

The computer hyphenates according to its internal dictionary and according to the rules of hyphenation programmed into it. This usually works out well, but it can hyphenate a word wrong now and then. If you have a word that is a problem for the computer, put it in the list after **.hw**. There is an additional problem you may run into: Words or word combinations that contain a slash (/) will not be hyphenated, whether they appear in a **.hw** list or not. If you have a word longer than the line length, which is admittedly unlikely, the word will stretch past the normal line length into the margin. However, within the word itself you can place "soft," or hidden, hyphenation symbols. These will not appear when you print out your file and will in fact be ignored if the word doesn't ever need hyphenation, but they will cause the word(s) to be split at the hidden marks if hyphenation is needed.

Here is the *hidden* hyphenation symbol: \%

Use it like this: word\%smith

If for some reason you don't want to use \% as your hidden hyphenation symbol, you can specify some other character to act as that symbol: **.hc** *\character*

You can use any character as your hidden hyphenation symbol but don't unintentionally use anything you commonly use within a word or it will be subject to splitting off. You'll probably run into fewer problems if you stick with the standard \%.

title: **.tl** *'left'center'right'*

Prints a title at the top of each page automatically. Just type between the single quote marks whatever you want to have printed as a title and it will be printed at the top left, top center, or top right, as you specify. You can leave the space empty if you like. If you would like to have page numbers printed and incremented automatically on each page, type a percent sign within any of the quote marks.

Dashes and Other Special Characters

Certain special characters are best made using these macros, especially when using **troff** for typesetting. They look better.

en dash: **\-**

In **troff** this produces an en length dash (–).
In **nroff** it will produce a single dash (-).

em dash: **\(em**

In **troff** this produces an em length dash (—).
In **nroff** it will produce a double dash (--).

one quarter: **\(14**

In **troff** this produces ¼.
In **nroff** it produces 1/4.

one half: **\(12**

In **troff** this produces ½.
In **nroff** it produces 1/2.

plus-minus: \(+−

In both **troff** and **nroff** this produces ±.

dagger: **\(dg**

In **troff** this produces †.
In **nroff** it produces either † or −, depending on your printer.

double dagger: **\(dd**

In **troff** this produces ‡.
In **nroff** it produces either ‡ or =, depending on your printer.

The -ms Macro Package

Here's a great example of the pluses and minuses of formatting with macros. If you use the **-ms** macros for title, author, author's institution, and abstract, you have the option of having them printed above the text on the first page and on a cover sheet, too; simply type the macro **.RP** at the beginning of your file. If you need two versions for different publications, a single **.RP** saves you two pages of typing.

But if you want a different style altogether, for instance, with the abstract by itself on a second page, you may not want to use those macros at all. Macros are most important when they give you options. When they allow you to make two (necessarily different) versions without retyping (especially with multiple authors), they can be a great time-saver.

Making a Cover Sheet

Request **P**age: **.RP**

Requests a cover sheet on which is automatically typed the title (**.TL**), author's name (**.AU**), author's institution (**.AI**), and abstract (**.AB**), if any of these macro command have been used. The date (from the computer's internal clock/calendar) will be automatically printed on the cover sheet unless you also use the command **.ND** (*No Date*).

TitLe: **.TL**

Prints the title at the top of the first page of text (and also on the cover sheet if you use the *Request Page* command, the macro **.RP**). The title is centered and printed with a 5-inch line length unless you use the *break line* (**.br**) command at the points where you want the lines of a multiline title to break. **troff** sets the title in 12-point boldface type.

AUthor: **.AU**

Prints the author's name, centered, below the title on the first page of text (and also on the cover sheet if you use the *Request Page* macro **.RP**). More than one author may be listed here, but if they are not from the same institution (assuming you want to use the *Author's Institution* macro, **.AI**) you may want to alternate author and author's institution listings. You can add as many authors as you wish, but of course if you want them all on separate lines they may not fit on one page. If you have a space problem because of multiple authors, especially from different institutions, you can type them all after this macro and ignore the **.AI** macro that follows. Each line you type after the **.AU** macro will be centered. **troff** sets the author's name in 10-point italic type.

Author's Institution: **.AI**

Prints the author's institution, centered, along with any other information you like, such as city and state, below the author's name on the first page of text (and on the cover sheet if you use the **.RP** macro).

Abstract, Begin: **.AB**

Begins an abstract, which is printed on a line 5/6 as long as the line length in the command **nr. LL**, which sets the line length (see **Number Registers**, later in this chapter). It also prints the heading "ABSTRACT," centered and separated from the abstract by a space. If you use the **.RP** command, the abstract will be printed on the cover sheet. If you don't use **.RP**, the abstract will be printed above the beginning of the text on the first page.

Abstract, Begin (no heading): **.AB no**

Begins an abstract printed on a line 5/6 as long as the line length in the command **.nr LL**. It is just the same as the command **.AB**, except that it does not print the "ABSTRACT" heading.

Abstract, End: **.AE**

Ends the abstract.

Headers and Footers

You can put these in or leave them out. They are used for putting in a title or page number (which is incremented automatically) on either the top or the bottom of each page. If you want to change headers or footers, put another set of header or footer macros on the page before you want the change to show up.

To have page numbers printed and automatically incremented on each page, place a percent sign after the command that designates the desired header or footer position: %

You can type anything you like after the appropriate header or footer command, as long as you want it printed on each page.

designate Left Header: **.ds LH** *desired header*

Prints in top left corner.

designate **C**enter **H**eader: **.ds CH** *desired header*
Prints in top center.

designate **R**ight **H**eader: **.ds RH** *desired header*
Prints in top right corner.

designate **L**eft **F**ooter: **.ds LF** *desired footer*
Prints in bottom left corner.

designate **C**enter **F**ooter: **.ds CF** *desired footer*
Prints in bottom center.

designate **R**ight **F**ooter: **.ds RF** *desired footer*
designate Prints in bottom right corner.

Paragraphs

Whether or not you use the cover sheet macros from the preceding section, you need to use a paragraph macro to let **-ms** know you are starting to format text. If you are typing your paragraph spacing and indentation instead of letting the computer do it, just use one **.LP** macro (described below) before the text, for **-ms**'s sake.

number **r**egister, **P**aragraph **D**istance: **.nr PD** *number*

Sets the distance between the preceding text and the paragraph and is automatically invoked when any of the paragraph macros are used. It can be set to zero if you don't want any space between paragraphs. Be sure to use your choice of measurement unit (**i**, **c**, **n**, **m**, etc.) immediately after the number when you set up a number register.

number **r**egister, **P**aragraph **I**ndent: **.nr PI** *number* **n**

Sets the number of spaces indented whenever any of the macros for an indented paragraph are used. Although I'm showing an **n** (en) here as the unit of measure, you can use **m** (em), **c** (centimeters), or **i** (inches) if you prefer.

If you are using **troff** to typeset your text, these paragraph macros will readjust the type size to 10 points unless you set a different value for type size with the point-size number register. The type style will also be changed to Roman (standard) type.

number register, Point Size:	**.nr PS** *number*
The default value is:	10 points

Sets type size – only in **troff**: 1 point equals 1/72 inch. Ignored in **nroff**. Don't use a **p** for ''points'' after the number or the computer will get confused and probably give you the wrong size.

Plain Paragraph: **.PP**

Both separated from the preceding text and with the first line indented.

Left-blocked Paragraph: **.LP**

Separated from the preceding text but not indented.

Identified Paragraph: **.IP** "*label*" *number*

Separated from the preceding text *and all* lines indented. It can be followed by a ''hanging tag,'' or label, which will be printed in the margin. The tag should be typed within double quote marks (" "); the double quote marks will not be printed. If you want the tag to contain double quote marks, you must use two sets of quotes for every set you want printed. If you want a nonstandard indentation, you can state this with a number after the hanging tag. Neither the label nor the indentation needs to be added. If you want a nonstandard indentation without a hanging tag, use a pair of double quote marks without anything typed between them.

number **r**egister, **Q**uote paragraph **I**ndent: **.nr QI** *number* **n**

Sets the indentation for your quote paragraphs only.

Quote **P**aragraph, indented: **.QP**

Separated from the preceding text the same distance as your other paragraphs and indented from both left *and* right by the amount set by the command **.QI**. If you are printing your other text double spaced but want the quote paragraph single spaced, you will need to use the single-spacing macro **.ls 1** or the **-ms** number register **.nr VS 12** just before the **.QP** macro. You will also need to change back to double spacing (**.ls 2** or **.nr VS 24**) before resuming your regular text.

Headings

Section **H**eading: **.SH** "*title*"

Separated from the preceding text by one space, left adjusted, and either underlined (in **nroff**) or in boldface (in **troff**). The title should be set between double quotes; the quote marks will not be printed.

Numbered Heading: **.NH** *digits* "*title*"

Separated from the preceding text by one space, left adjusted, underlined (in **nroff**) or boldface (in **troff**), and automatically numbered. The number is between one and five digits long and the digit specified in the command is automatically incremented.

Example:		
	.NH 3 "A Title"	1.1.1. A Title
	.NH 3 "B Title"	1.1.2. B Title
	.NH 2 "C Title"	1.2. C Title
	.NH 3 "D Title"	1.2.1. D Title
	.NH 2 "E Title"	1.3. E Title
	.NH 1 "F Title"	2. F Title
	.NH 0 "G Title"	1. G Title

Nesting

Nesting is most often used when you want several progressively indented subparagraphs, usually when you are making some sort of list.

Right Shift: **.RS**

Indents the number of spaces previously set in the number register **.nr PI** *number* **n**.

REturn: **.RE**

Unindents the text previously indented by the **.RS** command.

Using the **.RS** command several times without using a corresponding **.RE** command will cause the indentation to accumulate. To return the indentation to the original margin after using several **.RS** commands, an equivalent number of **.RE** commands must be used.

Example:

If this is your regular left-side margin,
        one **.RS** command causes this.
                Another **.RS** causes this.
                The next paragraph(s) will also have this margin,
        until you use an **.RE** command to move the margin back,
and another **.RE** command gets you back to normal.

Underlining and Changing Font (Type Style)

The commands that change font (type style) on a typesetter just underline on a printer. If you want to underline on a printer, you can use a macro like **.UL** on a line by itself, followed by a line of one or more words you want underlined. If you find it easier to edit on the computer if your text isn't split up into short lines, use the **\f2***word***\f1** command to underline a word or words within a block of text.

Changing Font: (Type Style)	**Font No. 1**	in **nroff** = stndard type in **troff** = Times Roman
	Font No. 2	in **nroff** = underlining in **troff** = italics
	Font No. 3	in **nroff** = underlining in **troff** = boldface

To change the type style temporarily: **\f2***word or words***\f1**

Be sure you use the **\f1** to return to the standard type style or all the rest of your text will be printed in the type style you changed to.

Italicize (in **troff**) or underline (in **nroff**): **.I** *optional.word*

Change to Font No. 2. If there is a word after the command, only that one word is changed. Any punctuation you would like after the word should have a space between the word and the punctuation; it will be joined to the first word. If another word is placed on the same line, it will be joined to the first word, but in the previous font.

Boldface (in **troff**) or underline (in **nroff**): **.B** *optional.word*

Change to Font No. 3. If there is a word after the command, only that one word is changed. Any punctuation you would like after the word should have a space between the word and the punctuation; it will be joined to the first word. If another word is placed on the same line, it will be joined to the first word, but in the previous font.

Roman type (in **troff**) or standard type (in **nroff**): **.R**

Change to Font No. 1.

UnderLine (in **troff**) or UnderLine (in **nroff**): **.UL** *word*

If the word is placed after the **.UL** command and on the same line, **.UL** underlines only that one word. Besides the word you want underlined, only one other word may be placed on the same line as the command; any other words on that line will be ignored. If **.UL** is placed on a line by itself, all following lines are underlined. You can shut it off with: **.R**

Boxing

BoX: **.BX** *word*

Draws a box around the following word. This works better in **troff** than in **nroff,** where the box must usually be made up of broken lines.

Box **1** (start): **.B1**

Starts drawing a box around several words or a passage of text. In **nroff** this will be made up of broken lines, so it won't be as attractive as in **troff.**

Box **2** (end): **.B2**

Ends drawing a box around several words or a passage of text.

Dates

Automatic Date: If you don't use one of the **.ND** commands when using the **-ms** macros, the current date (if your computer system's internal calendar is accurate) is printed at the bottom of the cover sheet if you are using **troff** or the **.RP** format in **nroff,** or at the bottom of every sheet if you are using standard **nroff.**

No Date: **.ND**

Suppresses the printing of the date.

New Date: **.ND** *date*

Prints *any* date you want, but *only* if you are using the **.RP** format and then *only* on the cover sheet.

DAte: **.DA**

Prints the *current* date (taken from your computer system's internal calendar) at the bottom of each sheet, including the cover sheet, in both **nroff** and **troff**.

DAte: **.DA** *date*

Prints *any* date you want, on every page, including the cover sheet, in both **nroff** and **troff**.

Making Columns

These macros are used to make multiple columns of text like those you find in some books or journals.

Making Two or More Columns

When you print this out, you will have to direct your formatting command through a filter program called **col**. That is explained in the next chapter, **Formatting and Printing**.

2-Column format: **.2C**

Switches to two-column format, with columns widths of 7/15 of the current line length (as stated in the number register **.nr LL**), separated by 1/15 of the current line length.

1-Column format: **.1C**

Switches back to one-column format (the standard line width). Also causes a page break, starting a new page.

MultiColumn format: **.MC** *column.width*

Switches to multicolumn format, making as many columns as will fit into the current line length. The column width must be stated as a number (it can be a decimal fraction) followed by a unit of measure.

Footnotes

Footnote Start: **.FS**

Placing this macro on the line before you begin your footnote will make it automatically save space at the bottom of the page and print the footnote. It also types a short line between the text and the footnote. This macro is especially handy for taking some text already typed and turning it into a footnote when you've decided that it's good info but a little complex for regular text. If your footnote is real long, it will be continued at the bottom of the next page.

Footnote End: **.FE**

This signifies the end of the text to be placed in the footnote and should be typed on the line after the footnote text ends.

Footnote Start, marking and numbering: **.FS** *character*

To mark your footnotes with any number, letter, or other character simply place that character at the end of the text *before* you go to the next line and give the **.FS** command. Then repeat the character (number or letter) just in front of the footnote text.

Since many characters are commonly used in regular text, it might get confused if you use a regular letter or number. A common solution is the asterisk: *

Others are the dagger or cross (†) or double dagger (‡), which can be produced by the typesetter **troff** with these commands: for dagger: \\(**dg**

for double dagger: \\(**dd**

In **nroff** these commands will work properly only if your printer is capable of producing a † or a ‡. If not, you will get: –

instead of dagger,

and: =

instead of double dagger.

In some versions of **-ms** you can mark the footnotes automatically.

Footnote numbers can be produced and incremented automatically if you place the following command immediately after the text preceding the footnote and repeat it just in front of the footnote text: **

The number will appear in brackets when you run off this footnote on a printer, but on a typesetter it will be a superscript, regular type one half line above the text.

Footnote Formats

Footnote Format: **.FF**

Used to set any of three optional formats for footnotes. If this command is not used the footnotes will have the first line indented and all other lines will be left adjusted.

To suppress footnote label superscripting: **.FF 1**

Puts the footnote label on the same level as the regular line instead of one half-line up.

To suppress footnote label superscripting and leave the first line unindented: **.FF 2**

To make the footnote come out like an **.IP** paragraph, all lines indented and with an optional label in the margin: **.FF 3** "*optional label*" *desired indentation*

How to Keep Text Together on One Page

Keeps, displays, and blocks are useful when you have text (usually a table or list) that you want to keep all on one page. This can't be done if the text is longer than one page, of course. Displays and blocks are macros that set off text to make it stand out. There are also macros listed here that make displays and blocks without trying to keep it together on a page.

Keep, Standard: **.KS**

This command does its best to keep the following text on one page. The standard keep will check to see if there is enough room left on the page being printed to put all of the text in between the **.KS** and **.KE** commands; if there isn't, it will not print any more on that page and will go directly to a new page.

Keep, Floating: **.KF**

Use this keep if it doesn't matter if the text or table immediately follows the text it is typed after. It also keeps text on one page, but unlike the **.KS** command, if there isn't room on the page to print the entire keep, it will print text from after the **.KE** end command until the start of the next page. Then it prints the text from between the **.KF** and **.KE** commands.

Keep, End: **.KE**

This marks the end of the text you began after either the Standard or Floating Keep.

Displays

DiSplay, Left adjusted: **.DS L** *optional.indentation*

A display is text that will be printed without filling in lines. Space is also left before and after the display (0.5 spaces in **troff**; 1 space in **nroff**). Any of these **.DS** commands also tries to keep the text on one page just as a Standard Keep does. If there is not enough room on the current page, the rest of the page will be left blank and the display will start on the next page. The letter after the **.DS** indicates the format, which in the case of **.DS L**, is left adjusted (and unindented unless you specify indentation by typing a number after the **L**).

Di**S**play, **I**ndented: **.DS I** *optional.indentation*

This display will be indented 0.5 inches on a typesetter or 8 ens on a printer. If you want to be ornery, you can specify some other indentation with a number after the **I**.

Di**S**play, **C**entered: **.DS C**

This display will have each line individually centered. Good for poetry.

Di**S**play, **B**lock: **.DS B**

This display will be centered as a block by trueing up the lines at their left edges (left adjusted), then centering the longest line.

Left-adjusted **D**isplay (without keep): **.LD** *optional.indentation*

This display will be left adjusted but no attempt will be made to keep it on a single page. No indentation will be used unless specified by a number after the command.

Indented **D**isplay (without keep): **.ID** *optional.indentation*

This display will be indented (0.5 inches in **troff** or 8 ens in **nroff**) and no attempt will be made to keep it on a single page. Non-standard indentation can be specified by putting a number after the command.

Centered Display (without keep): **.CD**

This display will have each line individually centered and no attempt will be made to keep all of the text on one page.

Block Display (without keep): **.BD**

This display will center the entire block of text by lining up the left edges of each line and centering the longest line. No attempt will be made to keep all of the text on one page.

Display End: **.DE**

This must be used after *any* Display command or the computer will think the rest of your text is all part of that display.

Changing Type Size in troff

LarGe type: **.LG**

This increases the size of the type by 2 points each time you use the command (a point is 1/72 inch). It only works in **troff** because the typesetter can change type size automatically and the printer can't. This command is ignored when you are using **nroff**.

SMall type: **.SM**

This decreases the size of the type when you are using **troff** (on a typesetter). The type size goes down 2 points each time you use this command. In **nroff** (on a printer) this command is ignored.

NormaL type: **.NL**

This resets the type size to normal. "Normal" means the size you have set in the **.nr PS** number register. This command is ignored if you are using **nroff** instead of **troff**.

Number Registers

Number registers are where the computer looks for values denoting the desired type size, line length, indentation distance, etc. The values of number registers are set with the commands on this page. They are usually set at the beginning of the manuscript, but don't have to be. They do need to be set before the macro commands that use them, though. Also listed are the "default values," the size or distance that is used automatically if you don't change it by using one of these commands. If you want a value *other* than the default value, just type the command with the value following it on the same line. For printers, which use **nroff** to format, only the number registers for line lengths, indentation, and other forms of spacing will have any effect, since letters are only one size, whereas for typesetters and laser printers, which can use **troff**, the sizes of letters can be adjusted, too. Of course, printers can usually use any of several print wheels or balls (for instance, elite or pica), but that option depends on your printer. The computer has nothing to do with it.

Units of Measure

A number register should have after it a number followed by a unit of measure, for example, **.nr PI 10n**. Otherwise you won't be sure what distance you're really setting. For instance, the distance could be set in "basic units," which are so small (1/432 inch in **troff**, 1/240 inch in **nroff**) that ten of them in the above example would not get you very far.

i = inches

c = centimeters

m = ems: a somewhat arbitrary measurement invented by typesetters;

on a typesetter with **troff** it's approximately the width of the letter *m*; in **nroff** it's equal to one space.

n = ens: on a typesetter with **troff** it's half the width of an *m*; in **nroff** it's the same width as an *m*.

P = a pica (1/6 inch)

p = a point (1/72 inch)

v = a vertical line space

u = a "basic unit," a typesetting measurement that is 1/432 inch in **troff** and 1/240 inch in **nroff**.

number **r**egister, **P**age **O**ffset:	**.nr PO**
The default value in **nroff** is:	0
The default value in **troff** is:	26/27 of an inch

This sets the left-hand margin by setting the offset from the left edge of the page to nonindented text.

number **r**egister, **L**ine **L**ength:	**.nr LL**
The default value for line length is:	6 inches

Sets the line length, and together with the page offset this determines the right-hand margin. You can use many of the units above to set the line length, but it will be easier to produce attractive formats if you stick with the same unit of measure whenever possible. I use inches because that's what I know best.

number **r**egister, **H**eader **M**argin:	**.nr HM**
The default value is:	1 inch

Sets the distance between the top of the page and the header, or the first line of text if no header or page number is used.

number **r**egister, **F**ooter **M**argin:	**.nr FM**
The default value is:	1 inch

Sets the distance between the bottom of a page and the footer, or the last line of text if no footer or date is used.

number **r**egister, **V**ertical **S**pacing:	**.nr VS**
Default value:	12 points

Sets spacing between lines in points. A point is 1/72 inch, and single-spaced lines (of 12-point type) are 12 points, double-spaced lines are 24 points, and so on.

number **r**egister, **L**ength of **T**itle:	**.nr LT**

The default value is whatever your current line length is. It sets the maximum length of one line of your title. A shorter title is centered.

number **r**egister, **P**oint **S**ize:	**.nr PS**
The default value is:	10 points

Sets type size – only in **troff**. Ignored in **nroff**. Don't use a **p** for "points" after the number or the computer will get confused and probably give you the wrong size.

number **r**egister, **P**aragraph **D**istance:	**.nr PD**
The default value in **nroff** is:	1 line space
The default value in **troff** is:	0.3 line spaces

Sets the distance that the paragraph is set off from the preceding text.

number **r**egister, **P**aragraph **I**ndent:	**.nr PI**
The default value is:	5 ens

Sets the paragraph indentation distance. Five ens is approximately the same as five spaces on a typewriter.

number register, Quote paragraph Indent: **.nr QI**
The default value is: 5 ens

Sets the paragraph indentation distance for quote paragraphs only. This indents all lines in the paragraph. Leaving it the same distance as your regular paragraph indent probably gets you the best-looking style.

number register, Footnote Indent: **.nr FI**
The default value is: 2 ens

Sets the indentation for the first line of a footnote. Set it to zero if you don't want the first line indented.

number register, Footnote Length: **.nr FL**
The default value is: 5.5 inches

Sets the line length *within* footnotes only. Set this to the same distance as your line length if you don't want your footnotes indented or shorter than text.

The -mm Macro Package

Making a Title Page or a Cover Sheet

TitLe:	**.TL**
Prints the title centered and in boldface, filling in unless you use the *break line* (**.br**) command at the points where you want the lines of a multiline title to break.	
AUthor:	**.AU**
Prints the author's name, centered.	
Author's Title:	**.AT**
Prints the author's title, centered.	
Abstract, Start (on cover sheet and page 1):	**.AS 0**
Begins an abstract that is printed on both the cover sheet and the first page.	
Abstract, Start (on cover sheet only):	**.AS 1**
Begins an abstract printed only on the cover sheet.	
Abstract, End:	**.AE**
Ends the abstract.	

Headers and Footers

These header or footer commands may be be put in or left out. They are used to print the title or page number on each page at the top left, top middle, or top right for headers and at the bottom left, bottom middle, or bottom right for footers. The 'left'middle'right' part of the command determines the position on the page of each header or footer entry. The command can contain a blank if you don't want anything written in that position, but all of the quote marks must be there. If you want to number your pages automatically, just put **nP** inside any one of the single quotes. If you would like to change the format of your headers or footers part way through the text, put the appropriate macro anywhere on the page *before* you want the change to occur.

Page Header: Print header on every page.	**.PH** " *'left'middle'right'*"
Even Header: Print header on each even-numbered page.	**.EH** " *'left'middle'right'*"
Odd Header: Print header on each odd-numbered page.	**.OH** " *'left'middle'right'*"
Page Footer: Print footer on every page.	**.PF** " *'left'middle'right'*"
Even Footer: Print footer on each even-numbered page.	**.EF** " *'left'middle'right'*"
Odd Footer: Print footer on each odd-numbered page.	**.OF** " *'left'middle'right'*"
To use an automatically increasing page number as part of a header or footer, place this within any of the single quotes:	**nP**

Paragraphs

number register, Paragraph space: **.nr Ps** *number*

Sets the distance between the preceding text and the paragraph and is automatically invoked when any of the paragraph macros are used.

number register, Paragraph indent: **.nr Pi** *number*
The default value in **troff** is: 3 ens
The default value in **nroff** is: 5 ens

Sets the number of spaces indented whenever any of the paragraph macros are used.

Paragraph, standard: **.P 1**

Both separated from the preceding text and indented.

Paragraph, left blocked: **.P 0**

Separated from the preceding text but not indented.

Headings

Heading, Unnumbered: **.HU** "*title*"

Separated from the preceding text by one space, left adjusted, and either underlined (in **nroff**) or in boldface (in **troff**). The title should be set between double quotes; the quotes will not be printed.

Heading, numbered: **.H** *number.of.digits* "*title*"

Separated from the preceding text by one space, left-adjusted, underlined (in **nroff**) or in boldface (in **troff**), and automatically numbered. The number is between one and five digits long and the last number specified in the command is automatically incremented.

Example:	**.H 3 "A Title"**	1.1.1. A Title
	.H 3 "B Title"	1.1.2. B Title
	.H 2 "C Title"	1.2. C Title
	.H 3 "D Title"	1.2.1. D Title
	.H 2 "E Title"	1.3. E Title
	.H 1 "F Title"	2. F Title
	.H 0 "G Title"	1. G Title

Underlining and Changing Font (Type Style)

Changing Font: (Type Style)	**Font No. 1**	in **nroff** = standard type in **troff** = Times Roman
	Font No. 2	in **nroff** = underlining in **troff** = italics
	Font No. 3	in **nroff** = underlining in **troff** = boldface

Italicize (in **troff**) or underline (in **nroff**): **.I** *optional.word*

Change to Font No. 2. If there is a word after the command, only that one word is changed. Any punctuation you would like after the word should have a space between the word and the punctuation; it will be joined to the first word. If another word is placed on the same line, it will be joined to the first word, but in the previous font.

Boldface (in **troff**) or underline (in **nroff**): **.B** *optional.word*

Change to Font No. 3. If there is a word after the command, only that one word is changed. Any punctuation you would like after the word should have a space between the word and the punctuation; it will be joined to the first word. If another word is placed on the same line, it will be joined to the first word, but in the previous font.

Roman type (in **troff**) or standard type (in **nroff**): **.R**

Change to Font No. 1.

Dates

Automatic Date: If you don't use one of the **.ND** commands, the current date (as far as your computer knows it) is printed.

No **D**ate: **.ND**

Suppresses the printing of the date. If you want to use this, it should be placed on the first line of the file.

New **D**ate: **.ND** *date*

Prints any date you want. If you want to use this, it should be placed on the first line of the file.

Making Columns

When you want to print out text with more than one column, you will have to direct your formatting through a filter program called **col**. That is explained in the next chapter.

2-Column format: **.2C**

Switches to two-column format.

1-Column format: **.1C**

Switches back to one-column format (the standard format).

Wide **F**ootnotes (while in two-column format): **.WC WF**

Allows footnotes to be full (two-column) width even while text is being done in two-column format. Otherwise, any footnotes will be the width of only one column.

Turn off **W**ide **F**ootnotes: **.WC -WF**

Footnotes will be the same width as one column. This doesn't need to be used unless you are changing back from the wide footnote style.

Make all footnotes on the page the same format as the **F**irst **F**ootnote: **.WC FF**

Footnotes on any given page will all be the same format.

Turn off **F**irst **F**ootnote style: **.WC -FF**

Pretty much self-explanatory.

Wide Displays (while in two-column format): **.WC WD**

Allows displays to be full (two-column) width even while text is being done in two-column format. Otherwise any displays will be the width of only one column.

Turn off Wide Displays: **.WC -WD**

Displays will be the same width as one column. This doesn't need to be used unless you are changing back from the wide display style.

Footnotes

Footnote Start: **.FS**

Placing this macro on the line before you begin your footnote will make it automatically save space at the bottom of the page and print the footnote. If your footnote is real long, it will be continued at the bottom of the next page.

Footnote End: **.FE**

This signifies the end of the text to be placed in the footnote and should be typed on the line after the footnote text ends.

Footnote Start, marking and numbering: **.FS** *label*

To mark your footnotes with any label, simply place that label at the end of the text *before* you go to the next line and give the **.FS** command. Then repeat the character after the command.

Since many characters are commonly used in regular text, it might get confused if you use a regular letters or numbers. A common solution is the asterisk: *

Others are the dagger or cross (†) or double dagger (‡), which can be produced by the typesetter **troff** with these commands: for dagger: **\(dg**

and for double dagger: **\(dd**

In **nroff** these commands will work properly only if your printer is capable of producing a † or a ‡. If not, you will get: –

instead of dagger,

and: =

instead of double dagger.

Footnote numbers can be produced and incremented automatically with the following command placed after the text preceding the footnote and repeated after the **.FS** command: ***F**

Footnote (**D**isplay) format: **.FD**

Sets any of a number of optional footnote formats. This way you can allow or prohibit hyphenation, make the right margin even or uneven, have the text indented or not, and have the footnote labels line up even with either the margin (left justified) or the text (right justified).

Sets no hyphenation, right margin even, text indented, with label left justified (this is the standard style used by **troff** if you don't use **.FD**):	**.FD 0**
Sets hyphenation, right margin even, text indented, with label left justified:	**.FD 1**
Sets no hyphenation, right margin uneven, text indented, with label left justified:	**.FD 2**
Sets hyphenation, right margin uneven, text indented, with label left justified:	**.FD 3**
Sets no hyphenation, right margin even, text not indented, with label left justified:	**.FD 4**
Sets hyphenation, right margin even, text not indented, with label left justified:	**.FD 5**
Sets no hyphenation, right margin uneven, text not indented, with label left justified:	**.FD 6**
Sets hyphenation, right margin uneven, text not indented, with label left justified:	**.FD 7**
Sets no hyphenation, right margin even, text indented, with label right justified:	**.FD 8**
Sets hyphenation, right margin even, text indented, with label right justified:	**.FD 9**
Sets no hyphenation, right margin uneven, text indented, with label right	

justified (this is the standard style used by **nroff** if you don't use **.FD**): **.FD 10**

Sets hyphenation, right margin uneven, text indented, with label right justified: **.FD 11**

How to Keep Text Together on One Page

Display, **S**tandard: **.DS**

This command does its best to keep the following text on one page. It can't be done if the text is longer than one page, of course. The standard display will check to see if there is enough room left on the page being printed to put all of the text in between the **.DS** and **.DE** commands; if there isn't, it will not print any more on that page and will go directly to a new page. Unless the **F** *(Fill)* option is used, a display will be printed as it is typed, without filling in lines. Space is also left before and after the display.

Display, **F**loating: **.DF**

This also keeps text on one page, but unlike the **.DS** command, it will print text from after the **.DE** end command until the start of the next page. Then it prints the text from between the **.DF** and .DE commands. Again, unless the **F** option is used, a display will be printed as it is typed, without filling in lines. Space is also left before and after the display.

Di**S**play, **I**ndented: **.DS I**

This display will be indented five spaces on each side unless a different amount of indentation is specified by using the Standard Indent Number Register, described below. Lines will be printed as they are typed, without filling.

Di**S**play, **I**ndented and **F**illed: **.DS I F**

This display will be indented five spaces on each side unless a different amount of indentation is specified by using the Standard Indent Number Register, described below. Lines will be filled, using words from subsequent lines to make up the desired line length.

number **r**egister, **S**tandard **i**ndent: **.nr Si**

Sets the distance that an indented display will be indented from both the left and right sides.

Di**S**play, **C**entered: **.DS C**

This display will have each line individually centered. Lines will be printed as they are typed, without filling.

Di**S**play, **C**entered and **F**illed: **.DS C F**

This display will have each line individually centered. Lines will be filled, using words from subsequent lines to make up the desired line length.

Di**S**play, **C**entered **B**lock: **.DS CB**

This display will be centered as a block by trueing up the lines at their left edges (left adjusted), then centering the longest line. Lines will be printed as they are typed, without filling.

DiSplay, Centered Block, Filled: **.DS CB F**

This display will be centered as a block by trueing up the lines at their left edges (left adjusted), then centering the longest line. Lines will be filled, using words from subsequent lines to make up the desired line length.

Display, Floating and Indented: **.DF I**

This display will be indented five spaces on each side unless a different amount of indentation is specified by using the Standard Indent Number Register. Lines will be printed as they are typed, without filling.

Display, Floating, Indented, and Filled: **.DF I F**

This display will be indented five spaces on each side unless a different amount of indentation is specified by using the Standard Indent Number Register. Lines will be filled, using words from subsequent lines to make up the desired line length.

Display, Floating and Centered: **.DF C**

This display will have each line individually centered. Lines will be printed as they are typed, without filling.

Display, Floating, Centered, and Filled: **.DF C F**

This display will have each line individually centered. Lines will be filled, using words from subsequent lines to make up the desired line length.

Display, Floating and Centered Block: **.DF CB**

This display will be centered as a block by trueing up the lines at their left edges (left adjusted), then centering the longest line. Lines will be printed as they are typed, without filling.

Display, Floating, Centered Block, Filled: **.DF CB F**

This display will be centered as a block by trueing up the lines at their left edges (left adjusted), then centering the longest line. Lines will be filled, using words from subsequent lines to make up the desired line length.

Display, End: **.DE**

This marks the end of the text you began after either a Standard or Floating Display. It must be used after *any* Display command or the computer will think the rest of your text is all part of that display.

Changing Type Size in troff

point Size: **.S** *number*

This controls the size of the type when you are using **troff** (on a typesetter). Standard is 10 points. In **nroff** (on a printer) this command is ignored.

Number Registers

Number registers are where the computer looks for a type size, line length, or indentation distance. The values of number registers are set with the commands on this page. Also listed are the ''default values,'' the size or distance that is used if you don't change it by using one of these commands. If you want a value other than the default value, just type the command with the value following it on the same line.

Units of Measure

The **-mm** macro number registers listed here don't need to use the units of measure used by number registers in the **-ms** and **-me** macros. Just follow the number register with a number, for example, **.nr Si 10**.

number **r**egister, **S**tandard **i**ndent:	**.nr Si**
The default value in **troff** is:	3 ens
The default value in **nroff** is:	5 ens

Sets the distance that an indented display will be indented from both the left and right sides.

number **r**egister, **F**ootnote **s**pace:	**.nr Fs**
The default value is:	1 line space

Sets the space between footnotes when more than one footnote appears on a page.

number **r**egister, **P**aragraph **s**pace:	**.nr Ps**
The default value:	1 line space

Sets the distance that the paragraph is set off from the preceding text.

number **r**egister, **P**aragraph **i**ndent:	**.nr Pi**
The default value in **troff** is:	3 ens
The default value in **nroff** is:	5 ens

Sets the paragraph indentation distance.

The -me Macro Package

Spacing for Top and Bottom Margins

Set vertical space or margin between top of page and header:	**.m1** *number of spaces*
The default value is:	4 vertical spaces (lines)
Set space between header and first line of text:	**.m2** *number of spaces*
The default value is:	2 vertical spaces (lines)
Set space between footer and last line of text:	**.m3** *number of spaces*
The default value is:	2 vertical spaces (lines)
Set space between bottom of page and footer:	**.m4** *number of spaces*
The default value is:	4 vertical spaces (lines)
These commands are usually set at the beginning of the text and then left alone. If you want to change them in the middle of your text, you must use **.ev** *(environment)* before changing the margins:	**.ev**

Headers and Footers

These header or footer commands may be be put in or left out. They are used to print the title or page number on each page, at either the top left, top middle, or top right for headers and at the bottom left, bottom middle, or bottom right for footers. The 'left'middle'right' part of the command determines the position on the page of each header or footer entry. The command can contain a blank if you don't want anything written in that position, but all of the quote marks must be there. If you want to number your pages automatically, just put a % sign inside any one of the single quotes. If you would like to change the format of your headers or footers part way through the text, put the appropriate macro anywhere on the page *before* you want the change to occur.

header: **.he** *'left'middle'right'*

Print header on every page.

even **h**eader: **.eh** *'l'm'r'*

Print header on each even-numbered page.

odd **h**eader: **.oh** *'l'm'r'*

Print header on each odd-numbered page.

footer: **.fo** *'l'm'r'*

Print footer on every page.

even **f**ooter: **.ef** *'l'm'r'*

Print footer on each even-numbered page.

odd **f**ooter: **.of** *'l'm'r'*

Print footer on each odd-numbered page.

Example:

Typing:

.ef 'Minimal Manual''%'
.of '%''Minimal Manual'

will give you this on the bottoms of even-numbered pages: Minimal Manual 1

and on the bottoms of odd-numbered pages: 2 Minimal Manual

and so on, with increasing numbers.

roman numerals: **.ro**

Makes your automatic page numbers Roman numerals.

arabic numerals: **.ar**

Changes your automatic page numbers back to Arabic numerals.

If you've started out using automatically increasing Roman numerals (for a preface or a foreword, for example) and want to change to Arabic numerals starting at 1 for your text, use the standard **nroff/troff** command for ''next page number equals one'' in the page *before* your text starts: **.pn 1**

Paragraphs

number **r**egister, standard **p**aragraph **i**ndent: **.nr pi** *number* **n**
Default value is: 5 spaces (ens)

Sets the indentation for **.pp** paragraphs.

number **r**egister, **i**dentified paragraph **i**ndent: **.nr ii** *number* **n**
Default value is: 5 spaces (ens)

Sets the standard indentation for **.ip** paragraphs.

number **r**egister, **p**aragraph **s**pace: **.nr ps** *number* **n**
The standard or default amount of space left in **nroff** is: 1 space on simple printers and 0.5 space on fancier printers.
The default value in **troff** is: 0.35 vertical spaces

Sets the space that will be left between a paragraph and the preceding text. It can be set to zero if you don't want your paragraphs separated from the preceding text.

If you are using **troff** to typeset your text, the paragraph macros will readjust the type size to 10 points, unless you set a different value for type size with the point-size number register. The type style will also be changed to Roman (standard) type, unless you set a different value with the paragraph font-style number register.

number **r**egister, **p**aragraph **f**ont italics (Font No. 2): **.nr pf 2**

Only in **troff**. Ignored in **nroff**. Only works on **.lp** and **.pp** paragraphs.

number **r**egister, **p**aragraph **f**ont boldface (Font No. 3): **.nr pf 3**

Only in **troff**. Ignored in **nroff**. Only works on **.lp** and **.pp** paragraphs.

number **r**egister, **p**aragraph **f**ont Roman (Font No. 1): **.nr pf 1**

Returns type style to standard Roman type. Only necessary if you've already changed the **.nr pf** register to italics or boldface. Only in **troff**. Ignored in **nroff**. Only works on **.lp** and **.pp** paragraphs.

number **r**egister, **p**aragraph **p**oint size: **.nr pp**
The default value is: 10 points

Sets type size – only in **troff**. Ignored in **nroff**. Works on all **-me** paragraphs. Don't use a **p** for "points" after the number or the computer will get confused and probably give you the wrong size.

plain **p**aragraph: **.pp**

Both separated from the preceding text and with first line indented.

left-blocked **p**aragraph: **.lp**

Separated from the preceding text but not indented.

identified **p**aragraph: **.ip** "*label*" *number*

Separated from the preceding text *and* all lines indented. It can be followed by a hanging tag (a label that will be printed in the margin). The tag should be placed within double quote marks (" "); the double quotes will not be printed. If you want quotes in the tag, use two sets for every set you need. If you want a nonstandard indentation, you can state this with a number after the hanging tag. When using **troff**, the label will be printed in boldface. Neither the label nor the indentation needs to be added. You will then have a paragraph that has all lines indented. If you want a nonstandard indentation without a hanging tag, use a pair of double quote marks without anything typed between them.

numbered **p**aragraph: **.np**

This creates a paragraph similar to the identified paragraph, except that it is numbered, and if you use **.np** paragraphs in sucession, the numbers will be incremented automatically. Very handy for a list of items, especially if the number of items you list may change in the future. The numbering will be reset when you use one of the other paragraph macros. Nonstandard indentation can be set with the **.nr ii** number register.

Headings

Of course, you can just type in a standard section heading. These macros simply do some extras for you automatically.

section **h**eading, numbered: **.sh** *digits* "*title*"

Separated from the preceding text by one space, left adjusted, underlined (in **nroff**) or in boldface (in **troff**), and automatically numbered. The number is between one and five digits long, and the digit specified in the command is automatically incremented.

Example:	**.sh 3 "A Title"**	1.1.1. A Title
	.sh 3 "B Title"	1.1.2. B Title
	.sh 2 "C Title"	1.2. C Title
	.sh 3 "D Title"	1.2.1. D Title
	.sh 2 "E Title"	1.3. E Title
	.sh 1 "F Title"	2. F Title
	.sh 0 "G Title"	1. G Title

indent: **.in** *number* **n**

Indents all following lines until you give another command telling it not to. You can use other units of measure besides **n** (ens), but use something.

temporary **i**ndent: **.ti** *number* **n**

Indents the following line only. Again, you can other units of measure besides **n**, but use something.

sheet keep: **.sk**

To make room for a full-page display that will be drawn or pasted in later. This will leave the next page blank except for any headers and footers you are using.

Underlining and Changing Font (Type Style)

The commands that change font (type style) on a typesetter just underline on a printer. If you want to underline on a printer, you can use a macro like **.ul** (only letters and numbers underlined) or **.cu** (all characters and spaces underlined) on a line by itself, followed by a line of one or more words you want underlined. If you find it easier to edit on the computer if your text isn't split up into short lines, use the **\f2***word***\f1** command to underline a word or words within a block of text.

Changing Font: (Type Style)	**Font No. 1**	in **nroff** = standard type in **troff** = Times Roman
	Font No. 2	in **nroff** = underlining in **troff** = italics
	Font No. 3	in **nroff** = underlining in **troff** = boldface

To change the type style temporarily: **\f2***word or words***\f1**

Be sure you use the **\f1** to return to the standard type style or all the rest of your text will be printed in the type style you changed to.

italicize (in **troff**) or
underline (in **nroff**): **.ul**

Only underlines letters and numbers, not punctuation or spaces.

italicize (in **troff**) or
continuous **u**nderline (in **nroff**): **.cu**

Underlines letters, numbers, punctuation, *and* spaces.

Making Columns

These macros are generally used to make multiple columns of text like those you find in some books or journals. When you want to print a file with columns, you will have to direct your formatting through a filter program called **col**. That is explained in the next chapter, **Formatting and Printing**.

2-column format: **.2c**

Switches to two-column format, with the columns separated by 4 ens.

1-column format: **.1c**

Switches back to one-column format. Also starts a new page, whether you like it or not.

column separation: **.2c** +*number* **n**

Separates columns by the number of ens specified. If this option is not used, the columns will be separated by 4 ens. You can use some other unit of measure if you like.

multicolumn format: **.2c** +*separation number of columns*

Makes whatever number of columns you specify, assuming that what you specified is physically possible. You can also specify a different number for column separation if you like.

As an example, to make a page with 4

columns, each separated by one-half inch, you would use: **.2c +.5i 4**

Columns will go all the way to the bottom of the page before starting the next column, so if you only have enough text for a half page, the right side of the page will be left blank.

break **c**olumn: **.bc**

Begins a new column, on the same page if there is room for another column, otherwise on a new page.

Footnotes

footnote start: **.(f**

Placing this macro on the line before you begin your footnote will make it automatically save space at the bottom of the page and print the footnote. It also types a short line between the text and the footnote. This macro is especially handy for taking some text already typed and turning it into a footnote when you've decided that it's good info but a little complex for regular text. If your footnote is real long, it will be continued at the bottom of the next page.

footnote **m**arking and **n**umbering: **.(f** *character*

To mark your footnotes with any number, letter, or other character simply place that character at the end of the text *before* you go to the next line and give the **.(f** command.

Then repeat the character (number,

letter, whatever) just in front of the footnote text.

Since many characters are commonly used in regular text, it might get confused if you use a regular letter or number. A common solution is the asterisk: *

Footnote numbers can be produced and incremented automatically if you place the following command immediately after the text preceding the footnote and repeat it just in front of the footnote text: **

The number will appear in brackets when you run this footnote off on a printer, but on a typesetter it will be a superscript, regular type one-half line above the text.

footnote end: **.)f**

This signifies the end of the text to be placed in the footnote and should be typed on the line after the footnote text ends.

How to Keep Text Together on One Page

Displays and blocks (''keeps'') are useful when you have text (usually a table or list) you want to keep together. This can't be done if the text is longer than one page, of course. Displays and blocks are macros that set off text to make it stand out. There are also macros listed here that make displays and blocks without trying to keep it together on a page. All blocks (**.(b/.)b**) and keeps (**.(z/.)z**) are separated from the surrounding text by one space.

begin **b**lock: **.(b**
(indented)

A block will begin a new page if there isn't enough room remaining to fit the text on the present page. If the options shown below are not used, the text will be printed as it was typed, without being filled or adjusted, and will be indented 4 spaces.

begin **b**lock, **L**eft justified: **.(b L**
(and indented 4 spaces)

The lines will not be filled but will be made to line up at four spaces in from the left margin.

begin **b**lock, left justified at **M**argin: **.(b M**

The lines will not be filled but will be made to line up at the left margin.

begin **b**lock, **C**entered: **.(b C**
(line by line)

The lines will not be filled, and each line will be individually centered. Most commonly used for poetry.

begin **b**lock, **F**illed: **.(b F**

Fills short lines with words from the next line. Can be used by itself or with the **L** or **M** options, like this: **.(b L F**
.(b M F

end **b**lock: **.)b**

Use this after the text when using any of the above blocks.

begin **l**ist: **.(l**

If you want to set off text in any of the styles shown above but don't care about keeping it on one page, use **.(l** and **.)l** instead of **.(b** and **.)b**, along with any of the options to **.(b**.

end **l**ist: **.)l**

begin floating keep: **.(z**
(left justified at margin)

Use this keep when it doesn't matter if the text or table immediately follows the text it is typed after. It also keeps text on one page, but unlike the **.(b/.)b** command, if there isn't room on the page to print the entire keep, it will print text from after the **.)z** end command until the start of the next page. Then it prints the text from between the **.(z** and **.)z** commands. The options to the **.(b** block command also work here. The standard form is unfilled text, left justified at the margin.

begin floating keep, **I**ndented: **.(z I**

Unfilled text, four spaces in from the left margin.

begin floating keep, **L**eft-justified and indented: **.(z L**

Unfilled text, left justified and indented four spaces.

begin floating keep, **C**entered: **.(z C**

Unfilled text with each line centered individually.

begin floating keep, **F**illed: **.(z F**

Fills short lines with words from the next line. Can be used by itself or with the **L** or **I** options, like this: **.(z L F**
.(z I F

end floating keep: **.)z**

centered block: **.(c**

This will not be kept on one page unless you use a keep – either **.(b/.)b** or **.(z/.)z** – on the lines just before and after it. It will fill lines unless you use **.nf** (no fill) and will center the entire block by centering its longest line.

end **c**entered block: **.)c**

begin **q**uote block: **.(q**

A quoted block is single-spaced, filled text indented four spaces on both sides and separated from the surrounding text by one line space.

end **q**uote block: **.)q**

Changing Type Size in troff

increase point **s**i**z**e: **.sz** +*number of points*

Increases the size in points – only in **troff**. In **nroff** (on a printer) this command is ignored. Don't use a **p** for "points" after the number or the computer will get confused and probably give you the wrong size.

decrease point size: **.sz** *-number of points*

Decreases the size in points – only in **troff**. In **nroff** (on a printer) this command is ignored. Again, don't use a **p** for "points" after the number or the computer will get confused and probably give you the wrong size.

point size: **.ps** *number of points*

Sets the size in points no matter what is was before – only in **troff**. In **nroff** (on a printer) this command is ignored.

Number Registers

Number registers are where the computer looks for values denoting the desired type size, line length, indentation distance, etc. The values of number registers are set with the commands on this page. They are usually set at the beginning of the manuscript but don't have to be. They do need to be set before the macro commands that use them, though. Also listed are the "default values," the size or distance that is used automatically if you don't change it by using one of these commands. If you want a value *other* than the default value, just type the command with the value following it on the same line. For printers (**nroff**) the letters are only one size and these number registers can't change them, only the spacing, whereas for typesetters (**troff**) the sizes of letters can be adjusted, too. Of course, printers can usually use any of several print wheels or balls (for instance, elite or pica), but that option depends on your printer. The computer has nothing to do with it.

Units of Measure

A number register should have after it a number followed by a unit of measure, for example, **.nr pi 10n**. Otherwise you won't be sure what distance you're really setting. For instance, the distance could be set in "basic units," which are so small (1/432 inch in **troff**, 1/240 inch in **nroff**) that ten of them in the above example would not get you very far.

i = inches

c = centimeters

m = ems: a somewhat arbitrary measurement invented by typesetters; on a typesetter with **troff** it's approximately the width of the letter **m**; in **nroff** it's equal to one space.

n = ens: on a typesetter with **troff** it's half the width of an **m**; in **nroff** it's the same width as an **m**.

P = a pica (1/6 inch)

p = a point (1/72 inch)

v = a vertical line space

u = a "basic unit," a typesetting measurement that is 1/432 inch in **troff** and 1/240 inch in **nroff**.

number **r**egister, **p**aragraph **s**pace:	**.nr ps**
The default value in **nroff** is:	1 line space
The default value in **troff** is:	0.3 line spaces

Sets the space that the paragraph is set off from the preceding text.

number **r**egister, **p**aragraph **i**ndent:	**.nr pi**
The default value is:	5 ens

Sets the paragraph indentation distance for a standard **.pp** paragraph. Five ens is approximately the same as five spaces on a typewriter.

number **r**egister, **i**dentified paragraph **i**ndent:	**.nr ii**
The default value is:	5 ens

Sets the paragraph indentation distance for ''identified'' paragraphs (**.ip**). Five ens is approximately the same as five spaces on a typewriter.

number **r**egister, **p**aragraph **f**ont italics (Font No. 2): **.nr pf 2**

Only in **troff**. Ignored in **nroff**. Only works on **.lp** and **.pp** paragraphs.

number **r**egister, **p**aragraph **f**ont boldface (Font No. 3): **.nr pf 3**

Only in **troff**. Ignored in **nroff**. Only works on **.lp** and **.pp** paragraphs.

number **r**egister, **p**aragraph **f**ont Roman (Font No. 1): **.nr pf 1**

Returns type style to standard Roman type. Only necessary if you've already changed the **.nr pf** register to italics or boldface. Only in **troff**. Ignored in **nroff**. Only works on **.lp** and **.pp** paragraphs.

number **r**egister, **p**aragraph **p**oint size: **.nr pp**
The default value is: 10 points

Sets type size – only in **troff**. Ignored in **nroff**. Works on all **-me** paragraphs. Don't use a **p** for ''points'' after the number or the computer will get confused and probably give you the wrong size.

number **r**egister, **f**ootnote **i**ndent: **.nr fi**
The default value is: 2 ens

Sets the indentation for the first line of a footnote. Set it to zero if you don't want them indented.

number **r**egister, **f**ootnote **p**oint size: **.nr fp**
The default value is: 8 points

Sets the point size for footnotes – only in **troff**.

Quotes and Other Special Characters

left **q**uote: ***(lq**

When using **-me**, it's nice to use this macro to make double quotes rather than just typing them; they will look much better when you typeset using **troff**. If you never intend to use **troff**, you needn't use it.
In **troff** this produces ‘‘.
In **nroff** it produces ".

right **q**uote: ***(rq**

In **troff** this produces ’’.
In **nroff** it produces ".

day of the **w**eek: ***(dw**

Prints the day of the week, from the computer's clock/calendar, which hopefully is accurate.

month: ***(mo**

Prints the month, from the computer's clock/calendar, which hopefully is accurate.

today's **d**ate: ***(td**

Prints today's date, from the computer's clock/calendar, which hopefully is accurate.

Chapter 7

Formatting and Printing

As I mentioned in the last chapter, there are two basic devices you can print things out on: printers and typesetters. They use two different Unix system formatting programs: **nroff** for printers and **troff** for typesetters. There is also a hybrid, using the formatter **ditroff**, which can produce typeset results on a laser printer, if the laser printer is capable of typeset style (usually the more expensive ones have this capability). **ditroff** has the same capabilities and limitations (as described in this chapter) as **troff**. However, as far as the person using them is concerned, they are the same program. Typesetters are neat for publishing papers and such; they are also expensive and impractical as a typewriter substitute. Laser printers that can make typeset style output are still fairly expensive, though nifty. Because of the expense, most folks won't be printing things out using the typesetter commands. Although the formatting programs (**nroff**, **troff**, and **ditroff**) are used to produce different results, they all work the same as far as the person using them is concerned. I'm using the term **nroff** in the formatting commands, but **troff** or **ditroff** can be substituted if you are producing typeset style stuff.

When you run your text through the **nroff** formatting program, you will need to add a printer code for the particular type of printer you'll be using. Otherwise the computer will get it all wrong. Your installation may have only one printer used for everyone, a "line printer," or there may be printers scattered all over. If the latter is the case, you will have to find out the right code to send your files to the proper printer.

Whoever is in charge of your computer center will have to tell you the code. They should have it in a computer file you can look up on your computer, if they are on the ball.

You can find a list of the various printer options your system has available by looking in the computer's "terminal library" directory. Type:

% **cd /usr/lib/term;ls[RET]**

If your computer center people are on the ball, they should have a file that tells you which code covers which printer. Chances are good their list will not be very exhaustive or necessarily self-explanatory. So if they don't explain what printers the various codes in the "terminal library" directory refer to, you will have to call them up and ask which code to use for your printer.

When you find the proper code for your printer, you can run your file through the formatting program using the printer code after the **nroff** command and any macro package command you are using:

% **nroff** **-***macro package* **-T***printer code filename* > *filename.rf* **[RET]**

For example:

% **nroff -ms -T***printer code filename* > *file-name.rf* **[RET]**

or:

% **nroff -me -T***printer code filename* > *file-name.rf* **[RET]**

By putting your formatted copy into a new file this way you will be able to check it over visually on the terminal and prevent wasted time and paper.

If you have used formatting macros to create pages with two columns, you will need to use the **col** "filter." Use it like this:

% **nroff -ms -T***printer code filename* **| col >** *file-name1* **[RET]**

Formatting and Printing Options

You can use any or all of these options in addition to any of the options already described.

If you are going to stand over a printer and feed it sheets one at a time (usually because you want to use good-quality typing paper instead of using regular computer paper), use the **-s1** option after the printer code like this:

-s1

While you are printing with a directly connected printer, your computer will be tied up. If you are using a continuous roll of computer paper, you can take a break. If you are using the **-s1** option and feeding in one sheet at a time, the printer will stop at the end of each page.

When using this system to print your file, you will need to restart the printer after you feed in each new page. To restart the printer:

[CTRL]d

If you only want to print certain pages, use the **-o** option. This is good to use when making references in a two-part process, as explained in the next chapter. It also keeps you from using more paper than necessary after making minor corrections in a file.

To format only from a certain page to the end of the file: **-o***page number* **-**

To format only from the beginning of the file to a certain page: **-o-***page number*

To format only from a certain page to another page: **-o***page number,page number*

This can be as involved as you like. For instance, you can format from the beginning to page 5, plus pages 7 and 12, 18 through 25, then from page 30 to the end by doing this: **-o-5,7,12,18-25,30-**

You can begin the page numbers at any number with this option: **-n***page number*

Sending a File to the Printer

The next step is to send the file to a printer. Type: % **lpr** *filename* [RET]

lpr is called **lp** on some systems. Simply try both and use the name that works. On a big system there may be printers in more than one place, and you will need to use a code with your **lpr** command to send your file to the right printer. For local information like this there should be a **help** file on printers and printing on your system. Look at **Help from the Computer** in **Chapter 9** for ways to look for a **help** file. If there is no **help** file covering printers on your system, you will have to call your computer center for information.

Chapter 8

Bibliographies

Bibliographies can be a pain. You have to check and recheck citations to make sure the title is accurate and the author's name is correctly spelled, and with multiple authors on papers and articles these days, it's easy to leave out one of the six or eight authors and then they're all mad at you. You need a hand. Maybe you can hire a good research assistant – but usually you get people who will cost you six or eight or ten bucks an hour, and when you finally get them trained, they go out and find a "real" job. No, what you need is a Unix system program to keep track of all your references, look them up and make sure they go into the text where you want them, *and spell those names correctly*.

You need **refer**.

With the **refer** system you can make a bibliography file that contains any or (ideally) all of the references you might want to use. This file becomes an electronic card catalog just like a library card catalog. You can add references to the file to keep it current and look up entries by typing one or more identifying words. For instance, once you have a bibliography file written, you can search for all the works of a certain author (as long as they're in the file), identifying the works by using the author's name (or even part of the name). The computer will find everything in your bibliography file written by that author and display it on the screen. You can simplify finding the works by using one of the bibliography categories to keep a record of where the book, journal, or paper by that author can be found. This could be the name of a library and the book's call number, or something like "third shelf from the top underneath the kitchen steps." The best part about using the **refer** system to keep track of your references is that you only have to write each one down *once*. That's it. for the rest of your life you'll have **refer** doing the dirty work.

The **refer** system was developed at Bell Labs for Unix Version 7, and it was improved at Berkeley to make it easier to use. So not all Unix systems have it. You can easily find out if your system has either the original or improved versions of **refer** by using the **refer** command followed by the name of one of your files. (Any one will do; this is just a test.) If you have **refer**, using the command on a regular file will make it print out on your screen. If you don't have **refer**, the computer will come back with "command not found." If you don't have **refer**, I hope you have plenty of time for proofreading bibliographies. Twice.

To find out if you have the **refer** system on your computer:	% **refer** *filename* **[RET]**
To find out if you have the newer Berkeley **refer** system, use the command **addbib** and follow it with a new file name:	% **addbib** *filename* **[RET]**
If you don't have the Berkeley **refer** system, the computer will reply:	Command not found
If you do have the Berkeley **refer** system, the computer will ask:	instructions?
If you are ready to start building up your bibliography file, you can begin. The computer instructions for **addbib** are pretty good, and I explain the system more fully right after this introduction. If you were just trying to find out if you have Berkeley's **refer**:	**[CTRL]c**

will get you out of **refer**.

The Berkeley refer System

The original version of **refer** is the stripped-down version of Berkeley's **refer**. I'm going to describe the Berkeley version first because frankly, it's nicer and easier to use. If you have it, use it. You will find the stripped-down version explained later, under the heading **The Standard refer System**. If you have Berkeley's **refer**, the commands in that section will work for you, too. First, I'll explain the Berkeley **refer** system of creating, sorting, and formatting a bibliography file. Then I'll show you how to create a bibliography file with the standard **refer** system. Finally, I'll show you how to place reference markers (numbers or names) in your text automatically and print the full references either at the bottom of the page, at the end of a chapter, or at the end of a book, with all the alphabetizing and underlining done for you by **refer**.

The Berkeley system of **refer** contains several steps: **addbib**, which you use to add entries to your bibliography file; **sortbib**, which sorts the bibliography file alphabetically; and **roffbib**, which formats the bibliography so that it can be run off. Let's jump in and take a look.

Using addbib

To start adding entries to a bibliographic file, type:	% **addbib** *filename* **[RET]**
The program will ask you if you want instructions:	instructions?
If you do:	**y[RET]**
If you don't:	**n[RET]**
Either way, the computer will ask you to type in your entries in a certain order.	

Example:	author:	*author's name* **[RET]**
	title:	*title* **[RET]**
	book:	*title of book* **[RET]**
	publisher:	*publisher's name* **[RET]**

As it asks you for author(s), title, etc., just type them in, then hit **[RET]**.

If any entry is longer than one line, be sure to type a backslash (\), with a space before it, before hitting **[RET]**: **[RET]**

If you need to skip an entry, don't type anything, just hit **[RET]**: **[RET]**

If you have an article or book with more than one author, the best way to type them in is to ask **addbib** to back up after typing in the first author:

author: *author's name* **[RET]**

The computer will ask for the next category, for instance:

title: **-[RET]**

You reply with a minus sign (-) because you want to let **addbib** know to back up (subtract) to author again. Then the computer will back up and ask author again. You can repeat this for as many authors as you like. When you want to go on to the title, simply type in the title instead of a minus sign.

Name Problems and Solutions

Remember, your computer is willing and able but not smart. When your author's last name consists of more than one word, the sorting and formatting process used later will think the last part

name is the whole name unless
: a trick. To keep a two-part last
together when you sort and for-
'ou use the command that stands
.he space that is no place,'' which
ıe spaces in the name:

\0

t in place of a space:

Franz de\0Waal

s will be sorted as:

de Waal, Franz

'**er** doesn't handle ''Jr.,'' ''III,'' or
.d.,'' as well as it should; it doesn't put in all the commas it ought to. See the examples in **Figures 8.1**, **8.2**, and **8.3** to see what it does do. When you are typing in ''Jr.'' or ''III,'' be sure to put a comma just after the last name. If you don't do it, the name will be inverted incorrectly and you won't be able to blame the computer. So type the name like this:

Chatsworth Osborne, Jr.

and:

Harry Cox, III

These will be inverted as:

Osborne, Chatsworth Jr.

and:

Cox, Harry III

The same works for an editor of a volume. If it is the editor you are citing rather than one of the articles or stories in the volume, the editor should be entered in the author (%A) category:

Perry White, ed.

This will be inverted as:

White, Perry ed.

You will see below that there is an optional **refer** code (%**Q**) that keeps the name in the same order it was typed. If the name has any spaces in it, use the **\0** space character I've described to fill those spaces. If you don't, **refer** will mess up on punctuation. The **%Q** code is described by Bell Labs as being for "corporate and foreign authors." Let me assure you that it works on any name you don't want inverted, even if it belongs to an American. I guess they just don't have any Americans with one of "them foreign-sounding names" working at Bell Labs.

refer Category Codes

Your computer may not automatically ask you for all the bibliography entry categories, or *fields*, that the **refer** program can use. You may want to make your own list for the computer to present to you. It's easy. I describe how to do it below. This is the way to go if your standard **add-bib** program doesn't ask you for the categories you use all the time. If you just occasionally need an oddball entry, you can add it in only when you need it.

To add a code occasionally, simply type a backslash at the end of an entry, just before you hit [**RET**]:	\\[**RET**]
Then you type the appropriate code from this list, leave a space, and follow it with your entry.	
CATEGORY	**code**
AUTHOR's name: This will be sorted with last name first when using **roffbib** or the **-a** option of **refer**. If the author has only one name *and is the only author in that entry*, use **%Q**. **%A** isn't set up to punctuate properly when given a one name author as the only author in an entry; it puts two commas after it.	**%A**
QUIRKY name: Use this if the "author" is a company or	**%Q**

organization or if you don't want the name sorted last name first. If the name has any spaces in it, use the **\0** space character I've described to fill those spaces or else **refer** will mess up on punctuation. Also use this if the author has only one name *and is the only author in that entry.* Otherwise, use **%A** for the author's name.

TITLE of book or article:	**%T**
JOURNAL:	**%J**
BOOK containing article:	**%B**

This is meant to be used only for a book containing an article. It prints "in" before the title. Use **%T** for the title of a regular book.

EDITOR of book containing article:	**%E**
SERIES title:	**%S**
VOLUME:	**%V**
NUMBER of volume:	**%N**
REPORT number:	**%R**
GOVERNMENT report number:	**%G**
PAGE number(s):	**%P**
ISSUER (Publisher):	**%I**
CITY where published:	**%C**

DATE: **%D**

OTHER notes: **%O**

To be printed at the end of the bibliographic entry. If you want punctuation at the end of your OTHER notes, you must type it in when you make the bibliography file. If you are using **roffbib** to format and print your bibliography file, this will appear in the main body of the reference. If you are using **refer** to put reference markers in the text and print the references, either at the bottom of that page or at the end of the chapter or book, the **%O** entry will be printed as an abstract, one line below the body of the reference.

KEY WORDS: **%K**

These will not be printed in the references but can be used later to look up entries.

ABSTRACT: **%X**

This is printed as an abstract only when using Berkeley's **roffbib** to print an entire bibliography file. If you are using **refer** to insert reference markers in text, the **%X** entry will be ignored when writing up the full reference, whether at the bottom of the page, or at the end of the chapter or book. If you don't want the abstract to be printed even you're when using **roffbib**, you can use the **-x** option to **roffbib**, which is described later.

Extra Bibliography Entry Fields

There are a few letters that aren't printed out by **refer**. These can be used for special purposes, such as telling you where you can find the actual book or article when you want to read it. The extra fields you can use are: **%Y**

and: **%Z**

You can add them to your bibliography file and put anything you like in them, such as extra notes you don't want to have printed or location information, such as library call numbers.

The Social Sciences Fix

There's another very useful thing to do with a spare **refer** field. When you use **refer** to put reference markers in your text, it always labels the references in the bibliography the same way. Is this dumb? Sure it is. Most computer programs are originally developed by programmers for themselves and other programmers, then modified for use by everyone else. When they modified **refer** to use the ''Social Sciences format,'' I guess they didn't look in many social science texts or they would have seen that the references in the bibliographies are usually not labeled in any way. Luckily, this can be fixed by using one of the extra **refer** fields. Doing this will give you the option of not putting labels in front of the entries in your bibliography. You will still be able to use the other options that label references in the bibliography.

But first a warning.

You'll notice that there are a few fields apparently not being used by **refer**. They are F, H, U, and W. However, the F field is actually being used by **refer** to store the reference numbers, so it should not be used in your bibliography file. Also, the H field is being used by the newer Berkeley systems as a place to put optional headers for the references, so don't use that either. You *can* use either U or W. You can even use Y or Z if you aren't going to use them both to keep other information in. I use W myself, so that's what I'll use in the description. You can use any of the unused **refer** fields I just mentioned as long as you are consistent.

Regardless of which field you use, this is what you put in it:

%W \&*

You're wondering what's going on here, right? The **\&** tells **refer** to use ''nothing'' as a label and the ***** tells it to swallow the period it was planning to put right after the label, whether the label was ''something'' or ''nothing.''

If you are using **refer** to automatically find and format the desired references for your bibliography and you don't want any labels on your bibliography entries, you have to have this field in each of your bibliographic entries. You won't have to type in the **\&*** part each time, though, because you can put that in more easily by using one editing command after your bibliography file is complete. Just put in the empty field:

%W

Then when you want to put the entry into the empty field, use either the **ed** or **vi** editor to make a *global* substitution:

:1,$s/%W/%W \\\&*/g[RET]

Because the backslash is often used as a special character in Unix programs, the extra backslashes are necessary to make sure that the computer realizes that in this case the backslash is supposed to be printed as a real character.

Now you have a special field in each bibliography entry that can tell **refer** not to print labels when it prints your bibliography.

If you want to print your bibliography without labels, you can now use the **-k** option to **refer**, followed by the field you are using:

% **refer -kW** *bibliography.-file text.file* **| nroff -ms >** *final.bib.file* **[RET]**

The **refer** program's *find* and *format* commands and all of their options are explained in **Printing Files with References Using refer**. I'll explain the use of the **-k** option again there.

With your ''no label'' field in place you can still use the standard **refer** command or its options to print bibliographies with labels of various types. But now you have the option of printing them without labels as well. Computers are *supposed* to give you options. That's what they are good for. We're just tidying up a loose end here, one that the programmers should have tucked in.

You can use any of these extra fields in a special category code file along with any other categories you want to have **addbib** ask you for. That feature is the subject of the next section.

Customizing addbib

If you would like to have a different set of fields presented for you to fill in, you can make a file and place in it the codes you want, like this:

desired prompt **[TAB]**-*appropriate code* **[RET]**

Example:

author:	**%A[RET]**
publisher:	**%I[RET]**
from where?	**%C[RET]**

Your desired prompt can be whatever you like, presumably it will have something to do with the category. You can put spaces or numbers or punctuation in your **addbib** prompts, but the total length, including spaces, can only be nineteen characters. Otherwise, **addbib** will only show you part of your prompt.

The only field you must leave out is the **%X** ''abstract'' field. The computer will ask you for that automatically, and if it isn't placed last on the list, **refer** will mess up the formatting. If you don't want to be asked for an abstract entry, just use the **-a** option:

% **addbib -a** *bib.file* **[RET]**

To use your own code file use **addbib** with the **-p** option, and follow the option with the name of the file that contains your codes before giving the name of your bibliographic file, like this:

% **addbib -p** *code-file bib.-file* **[RET]**

You can use both the **-a** and the **-p**

options when using **addbib**:

% **addbib -a -p** *code-file bib.file* **[RET]**

The **-p** option makes the computer print out the category prompts from your code file instead of using its own idea of what's right. You can list the entries in any order you would like to be asked for them. But no matter what order you have the computer ask you for the entries, the **refer** system prints them out in the order shown on pages 145 and 146.

sortbib

When you give the **sortbib** command, the file(s) you specify will be sorted according to the first author's last name, unless you use the **-s** option described later. Be sure to use the **\0** I described on page 135 between any spaces in that name or it will get split up in dumb ways. If some authors have more than one book or article in your bibliography, **sortbib** will then sort by date within the authors' entries.

To sort your bibliography, use the command **sortbib** like this:

% **sortbib** *filename* > *filename.srt* **[RET]**

That ''.srt'' attached to the previous file name is just my suggested way remember that it's a sorted version of the original. You can use any name you want.

Sometimes you will have a person whose name has appeared with several variations, perhaps because of marriage, for instance:

(before)	Goodall, Jane
(during)	Van Lawick Goodall, Jane
(after)	Goodall, Jane Van Lawick

Using **sortbib** will, of course alphabetize "Van Lawick Goodall, Jane" under V. If you want all her writings to appear in one place, you should always use the same last name. In Goodall's case, this can be done by using "Goodall, Jane" or "Goodall, Jane Van Lawick," and not "Van Lawick Goodall, Jane." This will not always provide a perfect solution, but at least you know of the problem and can take steps to avoid it.

You can sort your bibliographies by any field; the most common system has authors' names followed by dates, but you might want to sort another way – by date, then authors' names, for instance. Use it like this:

% **sortbib -s***fieldname filename* > *filename-.srt* **[RET]**

Here's an example. To sort by date, then author:

% **sortbib -sD+A** *filename* > *filename.srt* **[RET]**

To sort by date alone:

% **sortbib -sD** *filename* > *filename.srt* **[RET]**

You can go ahead and sort by any field you want. It's your bibliography.

roffbib

Then use **roffbib** to set the file up for printing. This will print ''Bibliography'' at the top of the page and do all the necessary punctuation, underlining or italicizing in each entry, except within the body of the (optional) abstract. Here's a sample bibliography file; **Figure 8.1** shows the **roffbib** printout of that file:

```
%A Author's Name
%T Title
%P Pages
%I Publisher or Issuer
%C City where published
%D Date of publication
%O Other notes
%X Abstract

%A Author's Name, III
%A Author's Name, Jr.
%T Title
%B Book Containing Article
%E Editor
%P Pages
%I Publisher or Issuer
%C City where published
%D Date of publication
%O Other notes
%X Abstract

%A Quirky\0Name
%A Author's Name, Jr.
%T Title
%J Journal
%S Series
%V Volume
```

%N Number
%P Pages
%I Publisher or Issuer
%C City where published
%D Date of publication
%O Other notes
%X Abstract

%Q Quirky\0Name
%T Title
%R Report
%P Pages
%I Publisher or Issuer
%C City where published
%D Date of publication
%O Other notes
%X Abstract

%A Author's Name, ed.
%T Title
%B Book Containing Article
%P Pages
%I Publisher or Issuer
%C City where published
%D Date of publication
%O Other notes
%X Abstract

%A Author's Name, Jr.
%A Author's Name
%A Author's Name
%A Quirky\0Name
%T Title
%P Pages
%I Publisher or Issuer
%C City where published
%D Date of publication
%O Other notes
%X Abstract

BIBLIOGRAPHY

Name, Author's, Title, p. Pages, Publisher or Issuer, City where published, Date of publication. Other notes.

Abstract.

Name, Author's III and Author's Name, Jr., "Title," in Book Containing Article, ed. Editor, p. Pages, Publisher or Issuer, City where published, Date of publication. Other notes.

Abstract.

Quirky Name, and Author's Name, Jr., "Title," Journal, vol. Volume, no. Number, p. Pages, Publisher or Issuer, City where published, Date of publication. Other notes.

Abstract.

Quirky Name, "Title," Report, p. Pages, Publisher or Issuer, City where published, Date of publication. Other notes.

Abstract.

Name, Author's ed., "Title," in Book Containing Article, p. Pages, Publisher or Issuer, City where published, Date of publication. Other notes.

Abstract.

Name, Author's Jr., Author's Name, Author's Name, and Quirky Name, Title, p. Pages, Publisher or Issuer, City where published, Date of publication. Other notes.

Abstract.

Figure 8.1: A roffbib Bibliography – nroffed

You can use **roffbib** like this:

% **roffbib** *filename.srt* > *filename.rf* **[RET]**

Or you could hook **sortbib** and **roffbib** together like this:

% **sortbib** *file* **| roffbib** *file.rf* **[RET]**

If you don't want to print the abstract, use this option:

% **roffbib -x** *filename.srt* > *filename.rf* **[RET]**

An option for **roffbib** that starts the page number for the bibliography at whatever number you would like:

% **roffbib -n***number file* > *file.rf* **[RET]**

Remember, tacking ".srt" or ".rf" on to the file names, as in the examples above, is just my suggestion to help keep you from getting confused. Use any name you like.

You can set some special formatting commands for your bibliography when you use the **roffbib** command by placing any of the following options after it just like the **-x** or **-n** options above. You can use more than one option after the command.

To number the references: **-rN***number*

To double-space all lines: **-rV2**

To double-space the references only, leaving the extra remarks (in the Abstract, or **%X** section) single-space: **-rV1**

To change the line length (the standard line length is 6.5 inches): **-rL***number* **i**

i for inches.

Alternatively, you can use **c** (for centimeters) or any other unit of measure, as described in the chapter on formatting.

To change the page offset (the standard offset is zero): **-rO***number* **i**

i for inches.

Or you can use **c** (for centimeters) or any other unit of measure as described in the chapter on formatting.

Now the bibliography is ready to be printed by itself. (Printing instructions are in **Chapter 7**.) You can also put your finished bibliography file (called here bib.file) onto the back end of your manuscript (assuming, of course that you've typed your manuscript into a computer file – the computer won't write it for you). I've dubbed that file man.file in the command description. Just use the command: % **cat** *bib.file* >> *man.file* - **[RET]**

The Standard refer System

The standard stripped-down version of **refer** uses a bibliography file just like the Berkeley version, but you have to type it up using ordinary typing and editing methods. You can use either the **vi** or **ed** editor, or just use the **cat** > command from **Chapter 4**.

To make a bibliography file with the standard **refer** system, start a file and type in any of the codes you need from the list below. Put a space after the code, then type in the entry:

%A *author's name*

%T *title*

Each entry can be more than one line.

CATEGORY	code
AUTHOR's name: Standard **refer** doesn't reverse the author's or authors' name(s) unless you ask it to. The option to use for reversing an author's name is **-a**, and it's described later. If the author has only one name *and is the only author in that entry*, use **%Q**. **%A** isn't set up to punctuate properly when given a one-name author as the only author in an entry; it puts two commas after it.	**%A**
QUIRKY name: Use this if the ''author'' is a company or organization or if you won't ever want the name sorted last name first. If the name has any spaces in it, use the **\0** space character I've described to fill those spaces or else **refer** will mess up on punctuation. Also use this if the author has only one name *and is the only author in that entry*. Otherwise, use **%A** for the author's name.	**%Q**
TITLE of book or article:	**%T**

JOURNAL:	**%J**
BOOK containing article:	**%B**
This is meant to be used only for a book containing an article. It prints "in" before the book title. Use **%T** for the title of a regular book.	
EDITOR of book containing article:	**%E**
SERIES title:	**%S**
VOLUME:	**%V**
NUMBER of volume:	**%N**
REPORT number:	**%R**
GOVERNMENT report number:	**%G**
PAGE number(s):	**%P**
ISSUER (Publisher):	**%I**
CITY where published:	**%C**
DATE:	**%D**
LABEL:	**%L**
The standard printout for **refer** numbers the references. This can be changed with options to the **refer** command. One of those options (**-k**) makes a label out of any entry field you wish; so use **%L** to create a special label if you want the option of having one.	
MEMORANDUM label:	**%M**

OTHER notes: **%O**

To be printed at the end of the bibliographic entry. If you want punctuation at the end of your OTHER notes, you must type it in when you make the bibliography file.

KEY WORDS: **%K**

These will not be printed in the entry but can be used later to look up entries.

Name Problems and Solutions

Remember, your computer is willing and able but not smart. When your author's last name consists of more than one word, the sorting and formatting process used later will think the last part of that name is the whole name unless you use a trick. To keep a two-part last name together when you sort and format, you use the command that stands for "the space that is no place," which fills the spaces in the name: **\0**

Put it in place of a space: **Franz de\0Waal**

This will be sorted as: de Waal, Franz

refer doesn't handle "Jr.," "III," or "ed.," as well as it should; it doesn't put in all the commas it ought to. See the examples in **Figures 8.1**, **8.2**, and **8.3** to see what it does do. When you are typing in "Jr." or "III," be sure to put a comma just after the last name. If you don't do it, the name will be inverted incorrectly and you won't be able to blame the computer. So type the name like this:

Chatsworth Osborne, Jr.

and:

Harry Cox, III

These will be inverted as:

Osborne, Chatsworth Jr.

and:

Cox, Harry III

The same works for an editor of a volume. If it is the editor you are citing rather than one of the articles or stories in the volume, the editor can be entered in the author (**%A**) category:

Perry White, ed.

This will be inverted as:

White, Perry ed.

Extra Bibliography Entry Fields

There are a few letters that aren't printed out by **refer**. These can be used for special purposes, such as telling you where you can find the actual book or article when you want to read it. The extra fields you can use are:

%Y

and:

%Z

You can add them to your bibliography file and put anything you like in them, such as extra notes you don't want to have printed or location information, such as library call numbers.

The Social Sciences Fix

Spare **refer** fields can be put to use to fix a problem you will run up against if you want your references unlabeled, as in most of the social sciences. This is done in the same way in either the standard or Berkeley versions of **refer**. Check the previous section on **The Social Sciences Fix**, beginning on page 139, for instructions on how to tell **refer** not to label your references.

Looking Up Entries in Your Bibliography File

As you keep adding your favorite references to a bibliographic file your researching will get easier and faster. Besides automatically placing references in your text at the proper places and printing out your bibliographies, you can look up references quickly and easily by using just a few words from the reference as identifying words.

Use this command: % **lookbib** *bibliography.-file* **[RET]**

The Berkeley system will ask you if you want instructions. You don't need them; it's easy. Just type **y** for *yes* or **n** for *no* and follow with **[RET]**.

On the next line type the identifying words: *identifying word or words* **[RET]**

This tells **lookbib** to look through the bibliography file for all references that contain the identifying word or words. They will be displayed on your screen. When the display stops, **lookbib** will show you an empty line. You can type another set of identifying words, or you can stop looking at **lookbib**.

To stop looking at **lookbib**, type a **[CTRL]d** on the empty line:

[CTRL]d

lookbib searches for the word(s) by making a special file with the name of your bibliography file and the suffix ".ig." This file contains words from all the bibliography entry fields except **%X**, **%Y**, and **%Z**. So when you choose words for a search, don't expect to find a reference with a word that only appears in the **%X** (abstract) field, for instance. The words are also shortened to the first six letters in each, the better to look for them. That's nice, but unfortunately you have to keep in mind that it also leaves out all numbers (except for year dates from 1900 to 1999) and all of the "100 most common English words," as determined by a list that **lookbib** checks before searching. You may be confused, for instance, if you search for a title by looking for the word "first." To see the list of words **lookbib** doesn't search for, type:

% **cat /usr/lib/eign[RET]**

The entries that **lookbib** displays on your screen keep printing out without stopping, so if you are using **lookbib** to find more than a couple references you can stop the action on the screen by using **[CTRL]s** to stop it:

[CTRL]s

Then you restart the screen printout by hitting:

[SPACEBAR]

You can also ''pipe'' the output through the **more** command so that the printout will stop after the screen fills up. You do that on the first line of the **lookbib** command:

% **lookbib** *bibliography.file*
| more[RET]

Then type in the identifying words as described above. After the screen fills and stops, you can print another screenful:

[SPACEBAR]

Or you can end your looking by first typing:

q

This will make the cursor skip to a blank line.

And then you type:

[CTRL]d

Pulling out Entries from Your Bibliography File

So you want to check some references. It might be handy to put certain bibliography entries into a separate file, then refer to that file at your leisure or maybe even print them out.

Putting Your lookbib Search Results into a File

You can pull out references from a large bibliography file with **lookbib**. If you want all the references by a certain author, for intance, or on a certain topic (looking for key words, usually), you can pull all the references that contain the identifying words and put them in a file: % **lookbib** *bibliography.file* > *file.of.references* **[RET]**

Then the identifying words: *identifying word or words* **[RET]**

Then finish with: **[CTRL]d**

Now you have a file containing whatever references **lookbib** found in your bibliography file. You can format them and print them, if you wish, using **roffbib** if you have Berkeley's system (BSD), or using **refer** with either the standard or Berkeley systems.

Placing Reference Markers in Your Text

Both the standard and Berkeley **refer** systems use the same method to place reference markers in your text. The standard markers are numbers, but you can also use a combination of the senior author's name and the date, a special label, or any of the other categories you put in the bibliography file. Reference markers are ordinarily surrounded by brackets by most printers or superscripted one half-line up by typesetters and some (usually expensive) printers. These features can easily be changed using command options described in the section after this. If you put two or more reference identifiers in a row without text between them, the reference markers will be separated by commas.

When you come to a spot in your text where you want to cite a reference, simply go to the start of a new line and type:

.[**[RET]**
identifying words **[RET]**
.] **[RET]**

The identifying words from the reference that you type can be from any category field in that reference. Usually you use whatever words you are most likely to remember, such as author's name, title, date, or any key words you used to describe the reference. You don't need to use complete names or even complete words, but there are three things you need to be careful about:

1. The computer will not print *any* reference if *all* the identifying words you use appear in more than one reference, so just using the author's name, for instance, may get you nothing except a computer message saying:

   too many hits

2. If you ask for a reference that isn't in your file *or* one that the computer can't find because you misspelled one or more of the identifying words, you get this message:

   no such paper:

   It will also tell you which reference(s) it couldn't find.

3. The other weird signal you may receive is the computer saying:

   :bad fgrep call

This means that you asked it to search for a word that is on the 100 most common English words list mentioned earlier. (**fgrep** is the name of the program that **lookbib** uses to conduct its search).

The trick is to give enough words so the computer can search the reference file until it finds just one entry that contains all of the identifying words. It usually isn't hard to do this. The author's name and the date will often be enough. Add in a word or two from the title and you have no problem. If you're not sure what word(s) you can use to differentiate two or more entries, use **lookbib** to look them up using the identifying words that got you the computer message "too many hits." It will print them all out for you on the screen and you can decide which words to use to distinguish between them in your text.

The standard reference form for **refer** is to print the reference as a footnote. If you want the references printed at the end of a chapter, paper, or book, type in this identifier at the desired spot:

.[[RET]
$LIST$[RET]
.] [RET]

Then you can use the **-e** *(end)* or **-s** *(sort)* options for **refer**. They are described below.

Printing Files with References Using refer

After you have made your bibliography file and put the reference identifiers in your text, you use these **refer** commands and their options to place your choice of reference markers in the text and make your finished bibliography. There are a number of different styles available for bibliographies. Even the options have options.

Here's a sample bibliography file and **refer**'s standard printout of that file; **Figure 8.2** shows the **nroffed** version and **Figure 8.3** shows the **troffed** version:

```
%A Author's Name
%T Title
%P Pages
%I Publisher or Issuer
%C City where published
%D Date of publication
%O Other notes

%A Author's Name, III
%A Author's Name, Jr.
%T Title
%B Book Containing Article
%E Editor
%P Pages
%I Publisher or Issuer
%C City where published
%D Date of publication
%O Other notes

%A Quirky\0Name
%A Author's Name, Jr.
%T Title
%J Journal
%S Series
%V Volume
%N Number
%P Pages
%I Publisher or Issuer
%C City where published
%D Date of publication
%O Other notes

%Q Quirky\0Name
%T Title
%R Report
%P Pages
%I Publisher or Issuer
%C City where published
%D Date of publication
```

```
%O Other notes

%A Author's Name, ed.
%T Title
%B Book Containing Article
%P Pages
%I Publisher or Issuer
%C City where published
%D Date of publication
%O Other notes

%A Author's Name, Jr.
%A Author's Name
%A Author's Name
%A Quirky\0Name
%T Title
%P Pages
%I Publisher or Issuer
%C City where published
%D Date of publication
%O Other notes
```

References

1. Author's Name, Title, p. Pages, Publisher or Issuer, City where published, Date of publication. Other notes.

2. Author's Name, III and Author's Name, Jr., "Title," in Book Containing Article, ed. Editor, p. Pages, Publisher or Issuer, City where published, Date of publication. Other notes.

3. Quirky Name and Author's Name, Jr., "Title," Journal, vol. Volume, no. Number, p. Pages, Publisher or Issuer, City where published, Date of publication. Other notes.

4. Quirky Name, "Title," Report, p. Pages, Publisher or Issuer, City where published, Date of publication. Other notes.

5. Author's Name, ed., "Title," in Book Containing Article, p. Pages, Publisher or Issuer, City where published, Date of publication. Other notes.

6. Author's Name, Jr., Author's Name, Author's Name, and Quirky Name, Title, p. Pages, Publisher or Issuer, City where published, Date of publication. Other notes.

Figure 8.2: A Standard refer Bibliography – nroffed

Figures 8.2 and **8.3** show a standard **refer** bibliography as it would be printed at the end of a chapter or book, using the **-e** option. If that option isn't used, each reference would be printed at the bottom of its respective page, in this same format, but ordinarily with fewer references than shown.

References

1. Author's Name, *Title,* p. Pages, Publisher or Issuer, City where published, Date of publication. Other notes.

2. Author's Name, III and Author's Name, Jr., "Title," in *Book Containing Article*, ed. Editor, p. Pages, Publisher or Issuer, City where published, Date of publication. Other notes.

3. Quirky Name and Author's Name, Jr., "Title," *Journal*, vol. Volume, no. Number, p. Pages, Publisher or Issuer, City where published, Date of publication. Other notes.

4. Quirky Name, "Title," Report, p. Pages, Publisher or Issuer, City where published, Date of publication. Other notes.

5. Author's Name, ed., "Title," in *Book Containing Article*, p. Pages, Publisher or Issuer, City where published, Date of publication. Other notes.

6. Author's Name, Jr., Author's Name, Author's Name, and Quirky Name, *Title,* p. Pages, Publisher or Issuer, City where published, Date of publication. Other notes.

Figure 8.3: A Standard refer Bibliography – troffed

For the standard printout, you use **refer** with the **-p** option. You always follow the command with the option(s), follow the options with the name of your bibliography file or database, and follow that with the name of the text file that has the reference identifiers in it. Then the whole thing *must* be piped (|) through **nroff**, **troff**, or **ditroff**, using the **-ms** macros, as shown here. Otherwise, you will get nothing. Finally, you send it (>) to a file you can look at (if you want to) before sending it to the printer. This is all done as part of one command, and the same basic form is used with added options to make bibliographies in other styles.

Putting References at the Bottom of the Page as Footnotes

For a standard **refer** bibliography: % **refer -p** *bibliography.file text.file* | **nroff -ms** > *file.with.refs* - **[RET]**

Putting References at the End of a Chapter, Paper, or Book

To put the references at the end of a chapter, paper, or book instead of at the bottom of the page: % **refer -e -p** *bibliography.file text.file* | **nroff -ms** > *file.with.-refs* **[RET]**

Putting References at the End and Sorting Them

To put the references at the end of a chapter, paper, or book and sort them according to the first author's last name: % **refer -s -p** *bibliography.file text.file* | **nroff -ms** > *file.with-.refs* **[RET]**

If you have more than one reference from an author in your bibliography, the sort option will also sort that author's works by date.

You can sort your references by various fields. Just put that field's code letter immediately after the **-s**. You can sort according to any field, but the most common is to sort by all authors within an entry, then the date:

% **refer -sA+D -p** *bibliography.file text.file* | **nroff -ms** > *file.with-.refs* **[RET]**

If for some reason you only want to sort using the first two authors:

% **refer -sA2 -p** *bibliography.file text.file* | **nroff -ms** > *file.with-.refs* **[RET]**

Inverting Author Names

If you want to write the authors' names last name first:

% **refer -a -p** *bibliography.file text.file* | **nroff -ms** > *file.with-.refs* **[RET]**

Some of your references may have more than one author, but you may not want all of the authors' names in that entry inverted. Just put the number of names you want inverted after the **-a**:

% **refer -a***number* **-p** *bibliography.file text.file* | **nroff -ms** > *file.with-.rcfs* **[RET]**

Printing Entry Fields in Caps

If you want a field (any field) to be printed in caps, use the **-c** option followed by that field's code letter (you can put more than one code letter after the **-c**):

% **refer -c***code letter* **-p** *bibliography.file text.file* **| nroff -ms >** *file.with-.refs* **[RET]**

Making Name/Date Reference Markers

The avowed purpose of the **-l** option is to produce references in the Social Sciences format, identifying the reference in your text using the first author's last name and the date of the reference.

Here's the standard name/date option for those who want the name and date as markers in the text *and* as labels in the bibliography. It also runs the name and date together, as in ''namedate'':

% **refer -l -p** *bibliography-.file text.file* **| nroff -ms >** *file.with.refs* **[RET]**

This option uses the same name and date combination as markers in the text and as labels in the bibliography. If this doesn't sound like the social sciences you know, welcome to the computer programmers' version of reality. You probably wanted the name and date to appear in the text and to have no label in the bibliography. This can be done with a few tricks. Look below.

Making References in a Social Sciences Format

If you want your references to appear with the name and date (with a space between them) in the text, and without labels in the bibliography, you need to use **refer** in two parts. First, you will run **refer** with the **-l** option described above to put the references markers in your text. To put a space between the name and the date you need to use the **ed** or **vi** editor to place an extra space in the **%D** (date) entry field and to remove it after you've put the reference markers in your text.

Then you run it with the **-k** option to make your nonlabeled bibliography. To use the **-k** option to make a nonlabeled bibliography, you need to use one of the entry fields described earlier in this chapter, in the section **Extra Bibliography Entry Fields**. And you use either the **ed** or **vi** editor to place a special set of symbols in that entry field.

To put a space in all **%D** entry fields in your main bibliography files, use the editor to make a global substitution:

:1,$s/%D /%D \\\0/g[RET]

This will place the symbol **\0** just before the date. It tells the computer to leave a space there. The extra backslashes are necessary in the substitution command because the Unix system often uses the backslash as a special character and one backslash by itself won't be printed. Be sure you leave a space just after the **%D**, too.

Then you use the **-l** option to **refer**:

% **refer -l -p** *bibliography.file text.file* | **nroff -ms** > *file.with.ref-.markers* **[RET]**

Now use the editor to return your bibliography file to its previous form with another global substitution:

:1,$s/%D \\\&/**%D** /g[RET]

Now you have a text file with name/date style reference markers and a weird bibliography. Don't worry about that bib; when it comes time to print the text, you don't need to print the bib. We'll print the bibliography from the next set of commands, using the **-k** option.

Use the editor of choice to make a global substitution again, this time to put something into one of your empty extra entry fields. I use the **%W** field, but you can use any of the fields described in **The Social Sciences Fix** section, beginning back on page 139:

:1,$s/%W/%W
\\\&*/g[RET]

All the **%W** fields will now contain \&*. You can leave this entry in your bibliography file. You can still use the other **refer** options to format your references in other ways with this entry intact.

Now you use the **-k** option, which makes a reference label out of any field whose code letter you put after the option. In this case we are telling **refer** to make a label out of ''nothing.'' **refer** will obediently comply:

% **refer -kW -p** *bibliography.file text.file* | **nroff -ms** > *final.bib.-file* **[RET]**

Special Labels for References

For special labels, you use the **-k** option without any code letter after it. This option uses whatever is in the **%L** entry field as a label. If you end that entry with a dash (-), **refer** will print a number after each label and increment the number automatically:

% **refer -k -p** *bibliography-.file text.file* **| nroff -ms >** *file.with.refs* [**RET**]

Parentheses Instead of Brackets

The easiest way to place parentheses around the reference markers in your text is to use another global substitution editing command, this time on the text file that has the reference identifiers in it. You want to make all the **.**['s and **.**]'s become **.**[('s and **.**])'s. Do it like this:

:1,$s/\.\[/\.\[(/**g**[**RET**]

and:

:1,$s/\.\]/\.\])/**g**[**RET**]

Since the editor uses the period as a universal search-and-substitution character (as described in **Chapter 5**), and the bracket is also sometimes used as a special character when editing, you need those backslashes to let the editor know that you're not looking for anything except those **.**['s and **.**]'s.

Now any of the **refer** commands and options will put the reference markers within parentheses instead of brackets (as on most printers), or superscripted one-half line up (on typesetters and some expensive printers). You can use other symbols besides parentheses if you like, but they are the most common.

There's nothing wrong with typing in the parentheses while you are typing the dot/bracket symbols in your text, but using the editor to do it after the text is finished gives you the option of doing your references both ways. This can be very handy when you're sending the same article to several places, each with its own preferred reference format.

You return your text file to its original form by reversing the form of the global substitution:	**:1,$s/ \.\[(/\.\[/g[RET]**
and:	**:1,$s/ \.\])/\.\]/g[RET]**

Chapter 9

Help from the Computer

You're all alone at your computer late at night. Your manual is at the office or the dog ate it, you're not sure which. The sweat begins to bead on your forehead, your breath is short, about six inches short of reaching your lungs. You're about to panic. What was the command you wanted? It's on the tip of your tongue, but when you stick your tongue out and read it in the mirror, you always seem to get it backwards. What will you do, what will you do?

Ask your computer for help.

The Unix system has a **help** program. It's just one of the ways to get help. You type **help** followed by the name of the topic you want help on. To find out what topics the computer will provide help information on, type:

% **help** *index* **[RET]**

If you see something that looks like a helpful topic, just type:

% **help** *topic.name* **[RET]**

Yeah, you guessed it. The catch is that the computer help files were written by computer geeks. They aren't sure what you want to know, so they assume you want to know ''all about computers.'' After all, that's what *they* would want to know in your situation. But hey, they're trying to be helpful; they just make things a little harder than you'd like. *I* assume you just want to get something done and are maybe stuck in the middle of it right now without **The Minimal Manual** and that's why you're having to ask the computer for help. Next time keep the dog away from the **MinMan**.

Some tricks for reading computer help files include:

1. Know what you want to do even if you don't know how to do it.

2. Be prepared to ignore 90% of what you read in the computer file.

3. Concentrate on the commands mentioned; when you see one that sounds as though it does what you want to do, look at the text explaining it.

4. If you don't skim well, if you like to read slowly, or if you want to skip back and forth while you are reading, put the contents of the help file you want to read into a new file temporarily. Then you can read it using either the **more** or **view** command, which allows you more control over the speed the file passes before you. This may also be a good idea if you have epilepsy, since some epileptic seizures are triggered by flashing

lights. This method avoids any possibility that trying to read rapidly whizzing lines as the computer prints them out on your terminal screen might trigger a seizure.

Here's how you call up a help topic and put it into a file.

To put a help topic into a file: % **help** *topic.name* > *filename* **[RET]**

To read it one screenful at a time: % **more** *filename* **[RET]**

To see one more line: **[RET]**

To see one more half screenful: **[CTRL]d**

To see one more screenful: **[SPACEBAR]**

To quit reading before you reach the end of the file: **q[RET]**

To *view* the file using **vi** editor commands to be able to skip back and forth: % **view** *filename* **[RET]**

To move around in the file, use the **vi** editor commands from **Table I: List of Commands for the vi Editor**, in **Chapter 5**.

To *quit* reading when using **view**: **[ESC]:q[RET]**

You can also pipe **help** through **more** to see a screen at a time: % **help** *topic.name* | **more[RET]**

There are two other commands on Unix systems which help you find topics.

They are **man**, which shows you sections from the **Bell Labs UNIX Programmer's Manual**, and **apropos**, which searches for a whole or partial word or phrase and shows you what section(s) of the **Programmer's Manual** has information on that topic.

To look up a topic in the computer's **Programmer's Manual**:

% **man** *topic.name* **[RET]**

If there is no manual entry for that topic name, the computer will tell you so. Then you use **apropos**:

% **apropos** *word* **[RET]**

The computer will come back with a list of manual entries that contain that word. You don't have to use a complete word, but the less specific you are, the more nonrelevant stuff you'll get back. For instance, typing "**apropos t**" would get you every subject containing a *t*, most of which would probably not have anything to do with what you wanted. Well, after you find a topic you want with **apropos**, use **man** to find the manual entry. You can put an entry from either **man** or **apropos** into a file of your own for easier reading just as you would for **help**:

% **man** *topic.name* >*filename* **[RET]**

% **apropos** *topic.name* > *filename* **[RET]**

Help with Spelling

Unix can check the spelling of your files. It prints out a list of any words that do not appear in its dictionary, including names or partial words and abbreviations. You have to determine where these words show up in your file and change them using editor commands from **Chapter 5**. Just type:

% **spell** *filename* **[RET]**

You can also put the words **spell** finds into another file and peruse them at your leisure:

% **spell** *filename* **>** *filename2* **[RET]**

There is an option to use if you want to check British spelling:

% **spell -b** *filename* **[RET]**

There is another option that doesn't show up in the manuals, so it may not be on all systems, but if you have it, it's helpful. To use it you make a file containing any words that you know are spelled correctly even though **spell** doesn't recognize them. The words must be one per line but don't need to be in alphabetical order. You can call your private dictionary file anything you want, but why not call it "dictionary," or "dict" for short? Then you use the spell **-p** (*private dictionary*) option:

% **spell -p***private.dictionary* *text filc* **[RET]**

For example:

% **spell -pdict** *text-.file* **[RET]**

Chapter 10

Hidden Files

Making Your Computer More Personal and Fun

One of the nice things about using a Unix system is that you can customize your computer to make it act a little nicer and more personal than, say, your typewriter or your toaster. You can make it give you a more personal (or less soullessly mechanical and threatening) prompt than the usual **$** or **%**. You can use it to keep track of upcoming appointments. Other changes will print a cheerful message on your screen when you log in, or print another file in which you can keep reminders like "Remember, the deadline is August 30."

You can make any file into a hidden file by putting a period in front of it. When you do this, the file won't show up when you use the standard **ls** (*list*) command. You will be able to get a list of all your files, including your hidden files, by using the **ls -a** (*list all*) command. So the only reason to use a hidden file is because you don't want it to clutter up your regular file list.

To change any of these files you use standard editor commands, using either the **vi** or **ed** editor system. Refer to that section of the book (**Chapter 5**) if you have questions on *how* to make a change. In this section I'll show you *what* you might want to change and *where* to change it.

First, use **ls -a** to list all of your files: % **ls -a[RET]**

The file you want to change varies depending on what type of Unix system you have. If your prompt is a $, you change the .profile. If your prompt is a %, go for the .login file. If the appropriate file isn't there, just make one and give it that name. Then use editor commands to put in any of the following lines.

To change your prompt, if your standard prompt is $: **set PS1=**"*your prompt here*"

If your standard prompt is %: **set prompt=**"*your prompt here*"

There are other goodies:

To make the computer display the date when you log in: **date**

To make the computer display a message: **echo** "*your message here*"

To make the computer display the contents of any file: **cat** *filename*

To clear the screen between commands: **clear**

To keep track of appointments and display them automatically on the day before and the day of the appointment, you make a file in your home directory and name it "calendar." Then you can put this in your .login or .profile: **calendar**

Now the computer will look through the calendar file when you log in, and it will print any lines that contain the present date as well as the next day's. This includes all of the weekend and Monday when you use the **calendar** command on a Friday. The date must have the month before the day or the computer won't understand it, but the month can be written out:

March 21

or abbreviated:

Mar 21

or a number:

3/21

Using the **calendar** option will make your logging in somewhat slower since the computer has to sort through the dates and this takes some time.

When you use > to put something in a file, you can goof badly if you inadvertently use the name of a file that already exists. The contents of the old file will be erased. You can keep from accidentally erasing your files in this manner by putting this line in your .profile or .login:

set noclobber

After you have put a command or a prompt substitution into your .login or .profile you have to make the computer read your substitutions. Ordinarily this will be done automatically when you log in, but you can do this without logging out and back in by typing:

% **source .login[RET]**

or:

% **source .profile[RET]**

Aliases

If your standard prompt is a %, you are in luck. You've got the version of Unix with the "Berkeley enhancements," and you can set up aliases in your .login file. These can be used to abbreviate often used commands or to help prevent you from accidentally writing over files and destroying them. And if you would like the computer to perform commands or display messages when you log out, you can put any of these commands into a file called .logout.

If you don't have the Berkeley enhancements, there is still a sneaky way to make some aliases. Read this section first, then turn a few pages to the section titled **Sneaky Aliases**.

To abbreviate a command, put a line in your .login file that contains the desired alias or substitute, followed by the command. Also on that line is the **alias** command, preceding the rest:

alias *substitute command*

A good thing to do with this is to make the remove (**rm**), copy (**cp**), and move (**mv**) commands "interactive." If you make the *remove* command interactive; the computer will ask you:

remove *filename*?

It will then wait for you to answer *yes*:

y[RET]

or *no*:

n[RET]

To make the **rm** (*remove*) command interactive: **alias rm rm -i**

The **-i** is an option to the command.

Making either the copy or move commands interactive will cause the computer to warn you about overwriting another file *only* if the new file name you want to use already exists. It keeps you from destroying the existing file inadvertently. The interactive version of the commands asks for a **y** *(yes)* or a **n** *(no)* just like the remove command.

To make *copy* interactive: **alias cp cp -i**

To make *move* interactive: **alias mv mv -i**

Another handy use of this function is to abbreviate often used commands. You can use any symbols rather than a simple abbreviation, but why go to all that trouble just to make things difficult to remember? Also, I don't know about you, but I hate to type any more than I have to, so I love to shorten commands. Here are some I like:

alias m mail
alias h help
alias ap apropos
alias c cat
alias v vi
alias vw view
alias mo more
alias so source
alias bye logout

You can combine commands using the semicolon to make one alias perform several commands one after another, but you should surround the commands with quote marks, or the computer will get confused.

Here's an example of a potentiallly nice alias that's a problem-child:

alias bye cd;logout

This returns to your Home Directory before logging out. But having this in your .login file will cause the computer to log out whenever you try to log in. Not a happy situation.

If this sort of thing happens to you, here's what you do. Begin to log in, and after you've told the computer what terminal you're using and it begins to react, hit:

[CTRL]c

This will stop the computer from reading the **logout** command in your .login file. You will then be able to edit the offending alias out of the file and log out, after which you can log in normally. Then you go back into your .login file and redo the alias, like so:

alias bye 'cd;logout'

All of these alias commands can be put in a file named .cshrc instead of in your .login file. For simple commands like these there is very little difference to you in using either file. If you want to use the .cshrc file, just make a file with that name if you don't have one already.

Sneaky Aliases

Without the Berkeley enhancements you can't make aliases. But you can make something that works pretty much the same. It's a computer program – **don't worry** – I'm talking about an *extremely simple* computer program.

I'll use as an example making the command **rm** interactive. First, make a file with whatever name you would like to use for your command: **remove**

In the file write the command you would like to use, in this case: **rm -i**

Now exit your file and prepare to make it "executable" by *changing mode*, like this: **chmod +x** ***filename***

In this case: **chmod +x remove**

Now your remove file can be used as a program; when you type **remove**, it will act as if you typed **rm -i**. But right now it will only work when you are in the same directory as your command. Not too useful, but that can be changed. First, make a directory, any directory, where you would like to store your programs. A common convention is to call it **bin**, after the "bin" directories that Unix systems use to store programs. Put it into your home directory, and put your program file into it. Got it? Okay, now you need to put something into your .login file – that path name for your bin directory. Find it by typing: % **pwd[RET]**

The computer will show you something along the lines of: /c/q/minman

Remember that. Find out whether your path name is in a .login or .profile file. It'll be one of the two; just see which you have by typing: % **ls -a[RET]**

Now use the editor to get into your .login or .profile file. I'll use .login as my example: % **vi .login[RET]**

Look for a line in there that starts with: set path

That line tells the computer where to look for programs. On that line are a number of paths to directories that contain programs. You need to add your bin directory to the queue. Just treat each path as a separate word and add your bin path name to it: **/c/q/minman/bin**

Write and quit your .login file. Now you have to make the computer read your new set of paths. Ordinarily this will be done automatically when you log in but you can do this without logging out and back in by typing: % **source .login[RET]**

or: % **source .profile[RET]**

Now you will be able to type **remove** from any of your directories and it'll be as if you were typing **rm -i**. But this might not be the most useful command substitution you can make, because the same method works for more complex commands that can be annoying to type and/or to remember. One more example:

nroff -ms \!* | lpr -T*printer option* **&[RET]**

Using this as an alias or as a program allows you to format a file and send it off to the printer using a shorter command name that is easier to remember. The \!* indicates that you will be typing a file name after the program or alias name you give to that line. Just put the line in a program file as described above or make it an alias:

alias *alias.name* **nroff -ms \!* | lpr -T***printer option* **&[RET]**

Either way, you're set.

Another excellent alias is for the **find** command, which can be fairly long and awkward to type. It was described back in **Chapter 4** and looks through all your directories for the file you ask for. Here's the alias:

alias *alias.name* **"find . -name '\!*' -print"**

Chapter 11

Emergency Relief

Suppose you've gotten yourself into some part of the computer that you don't know, and you don't know how to get out. **DON'T WORRY!** There is always a way out. Try one of these. If it doesn't work in the situation you're in, try another.

Good multipurpose commands:	**q[RET]**
or:	**q![RET]**
a perennial favorite:	**[CTRL]c**
or:	**[CTRL]d**
possibly:	**bye**
or:	**bye!**

Or my personal last-ditch favorite, which is to switch off the SOB.

The **[CTRL]c** may slightly addle the computer, but you can easily restore its composure by sending it through its login cycle again. You can log out and back in to do this, but you don't have to. Do this instead.

Get back to your home directory: % **cd[RET]**

And send the computer through its login cycle: % **source .login[RET]**

This makes the computer read the .login file and set its functions according to the settings contained there.

You will then be back at your home directory, just as if you had just logged in. You can string those commands together if you want to: % **cd;source .login[RET]**

Recovering a File

If you were editing a file and you switched off the terminal (either deliberately or accidentally) or pulled the plug (or hung up the phone if you are using a remote system with a phone modem), you will have to recover your file. If you have the **vi** editor on your system, it's easy, and it usually also works if the problem was main computer failure instead of your simply switching off your terminal. If you only have the **ed** editor in such a situation, you are out of luck.

Type: % **vi -r** *filename* **[RET]**

This will recover the file and place you in the editing mode. Just in case the file was only partially saved (which should only happen if the main computer "crashed," or broke down), you will want to write the recovered file out with a new file name so that the old version of the file is saved, too. Type: **[ESC]:w** *filename2* **[RET]**

Then: **:q[RET]**

This way you have both the file you recovered and the version without the changes you were making before the accident.

Chapter 12

List of Unix Commands

This chapter lists the Unix system commands described in **The Minimal Manual**. Most have a brief description after them, as well as page numbers for more information on that command. The commands are listed in the following order:

Commands With Prompt

Commands Without Prompt

Control ([**CTRL**]) Commands

vi Editor Commands

ed Editor Commands

Standard **nroff/troff** Macro Commands

-ms Macro Commands

-mm Macro Commands

-me Macro Commands

nroff, **troff**, and **ditroff** Commands

refer Commands

Commands with Prompt

Commands without Prompt

Control ([**CTRL**]) Commands

vi Editor Commands

ed Editor Commands

Standard **nroff/troff** Macro Commands

-ms Macro Commands

-mm Macro Commands

-me Macro Commands

nroff and **troff** Commands

Although only **nroff** is listed below, the options shown work with **troff** (and its variant, **ditroff**) as well.

refer Commands

Chapter 13

Conclusion: A Bridge to More with Unix

Most folks will be happy not to have to learn any more than what has been covered in this manual. Some folks will have to learn more because they want to do graphics for design or statistical analysis or typeset mathematical treatises. Some will even *want* to learn more. I hope each of you will remember that there *is* no accounting for other people's tastes. For those to whom this book is only a beginning, remember **man** and **apropos** are only a few keys away. Refer to the official **UNIX Programmer's Manual** and go to the library and get a couple of different books on the Unix system (use one book's information to help fill the holes in the other). They will be your guide as you move step by slip into the world of oral tradition, computer self-help, and big-time computer programming.

The **UNIX Programmer's Manuals, Volumes 1 and 2**, are a good deal because they are complete. They just don't tell you very well how to do the command they've just described. That's where the oral tradition comes in. "Oral tradition," when used by computer programmers, means "we don't know how to write a manual about it." It also means they like company, and mostly they enjoy sharing ideas and techniques with other people who like computers as they do. So ask. Self-help means use other books on Unix along with the computer's own on-line version of the programmer's manual to figure out what you think you can do with a Unix command. Then try it, and see if it did what you wanted it to. Self-help is the key to that big-time computer programming, because when you get to the point where you're trying to do something that the big kids don't think can be done, you are on your own. If you'd like to be able to do more with the Unix system, but you want the kind of help this manual gives you, don't worry. I'll be back.

Glossary

\0: ``Unfillable space.'' Tells the computer that there should be a space where this symbol appears while fooling it into treating two words as one word. Especially useful when sorting two word names.

adjust: Adjusting text is done by the printer or typesetter by putting more space between words.

alias: If your Unix system has the Berkeley ``C-shell,'' you can use aliases to make the computer accept a letter or word as shorthand for another (presumably longer) command or series of commands. It's actually a very simple way to make a short computer program.

baud rate: The speed at which your terminal communicates with the computer. The faster it communicates, the quicker the computer and terminal will display your commands and the computer's reactions.

Berkeley enhancements: Changes made by the University of California at Berkeley; they include things like the **vi** editor. Some of these (especially the **vi** editor) have been incorporated into many Unix systems.

blocks: Text you want set off from regular text in some way. When centering a block of text, the longest line of text will be centered and the rest of that block of text will be lined up at its left edge.

break: Used to break the current line, column, or page, and therefore to begin a new one.

buffer: A buffer is a section of short-term computer memory set aside for specific reason. Usually it is that section of text you are viewing or working on, or parts of that text you have deleted (erased from your screen) or yanked (duplicated) while editing.

cat: Short for *concatenate*, which means "to link together." It's used to link together stored characters in a file so that you can see them.

clock/calendar, Unix's internal: This is used to label file changes by time and date to help you keep track of changes; it can also be used to put dates on manuscripts or memos. It is set or reset when the main computer (not your terminal) is turned on. On a personal computer, you must reset the time and date each time you log in *if* you want the date to be accurate. On a large system the computer is left running for days and it's the responsibility of the system administrator to be sure the clock/calendar is set properly.

computer: A box of short-term memory that, when equipped with explicit instructions, or "programs," can be more useful than a typewriter or a calculator, if you keep your wits about you.

computer center: If you have a Unix system on a microcomputer, then you are the computer center. More likely there is a remote computer or two (or more) and the computer center is an office, offices, or even a whole building containing computers, printers, and a lot of slightly wacked-out humans (computer people).

crash, computer: A computer breakdown is called a "crash."

cursor: A little box, line, or blinking light that marks your place on the screen. Most new terminals have some way to change the style of cursor if you don't like what it is now. I, for instance, can't stand cursors that blink, but some people like them.

date: The date is reset whenever the computer is turned on. You won't need to do this each time you log in (unless you are using a personal computer) because large computer systems have someone else turning the computer on and off and it's usually on for days at a time.

dictionary, internal: The Unix system has a built-in dictionary used for finding incorrect spelling and for hyphenating words when formatting.

disk: Your files are stored on a disk. When you give a command to look at or work on one of your files, a copy is pulled from the disk into a buffer (short-term memory inside the computer) so that it can be displayed on your terminal screen. If you are editing the file, the edited changes you make are not written onto the disk-stored copy until you give a command to do so (**:w** for *write*). Because of this, if you make mistakes while editing, you will still have the version stored on the disk to return to. But you should periodically use the *write* command during your editing so that most of your changes will be stored on the disk, just in case something happens to your terminal or the main computer while you are editing.

displays: Text you want to be set off from regular text in some way.

dump: The act of copying the files from the disk to a long term storage medium, usually tape.

echo: A command to display a message, often when logging in or out.

editor: Much the same as "word processor" (editing plus formatting makes up word processing), but like most non-computer words compared to computer words, it's more accurate. A set of commands that lets you add or remove letters, words, or lines, or move them around or duplicate them, in general giving you the freedom to make more mistakes per hour than ever before. Go easy with a computer editor and it can be very useful, just like a human editor.

field: Within a database (an information storage system like an electronic card file) each entry is called a field.

files, hidden: Files that don't show up when you use the **ls** (list) command unless you add the **-a** option (list all). Hidden files are usually used for creating custom features.

filled text: When the formatting commands you use specify filled text the specified line length is made up with words from the next line until the formatting command is countered with another command. Filling doesn't necessarily create perfectly even edges on both margins. To do that you must use another command to "adjust" text.

filter: A program that you run text or data through to produce some sort of change. When formatting text with commands for columns, you run it through the **col** filter.

font: Type style.

footer: A label at the bottom of the page, usually on more than one page. Often consists of the page number and/or author's name, title, date, etc. The page number or date can be automatically incremented or updated by the computer.

garbage: Unwanted characters that show up on your screen are called "garbage." The usual cause is a loose connection somewhere between your terminal and the computer.

hanging tag: A label in the margin of a paragraph that has all of its lines indented.

hard-wire connection: A direct connection from your terminal to the main computer.

headcrash: The dreaded headcrash consists of the recording head of the disk drive actually touching the disk, a no-no that results in the loss and/or scrambling of information on that disk. The recording head is necessarily real close to the surface of the disk, so headcrashes can happen more often than anyone would like. That's why they make backup systems to store files.

header: A label at the top of the page, usually on more than one page. Often consists of the page number and/or author's name, title, date, etc. The page number or date can be automatically incremented or updated by the computer.

header margin: The space between the top of the page and the header, or the first line of text if no header is used.

home directory: The first directory you enter when you log in on a Unix system.

interactive commands: Commands that talk back to you, usually to ask if you really want to do what you asked, for instance when you're removing a file. Especially good for avoiding wiping out files by mistake.

keeps: Formatting commands that try their best to keep a group of text together on one page. If you've got two pages of text, a keep will not fit it on one page; the text will begin on a page by itself.

keyboard: Like a typewriter keyboard with a few extra keys.

laser printer: A printer that uses the same basic principles as a copy machine. Some laser printers can produce pretty good typeset-style printouts, although not as good quality as real phototypesetters. Laser printers cost about 10% as much as phototypesetters, though.

length, line: The important thing to remember about setting the line length is that together with the page offset setting, it determines the right-side margin.

lightning: Watch out! Your computer doesn't like it. Unplug your computer or terminal when you are not using it, especially if thunderstorms are likely.

line printer: A printer usable by all people on the system; it's usually at whatever location the computers are.

logging in: Connecting to the computer.

logging out: Disconnecting from the computer.

.login: A hidden file useful for customizing Unix to suit you. See **Chapter 10, Hidden Files**.

m: em: an arbitrary measurement used by typesetters. It is approximately the width of the letter *m*.

main-frame computer:
A large computer (which usually has a number of people using it) is called a main-frame computer. Somewhat smaller computers are called minicomputers, and personal computers are called microcomputers. Computer people get bent out of shape if you use the wrong word for a type of computer, but nobody else worries about it.

margin, bottom:
The space between the bottom of the page and the footer, if any, or the last line of text can be set the way you want. Also, the space between the footer and the last line of text.

margin, top: The space between the top of the page and the header, if any, or the text can be set the way you want. Also the space between the header and the first line of text.

mbox: mbox, or mailbox, is a file used on many systems to collect and store your mail automatically after you've read it, unless you specify that you'd like to do something else with it.

memory: There's short-term and there's long-term memory. Short-term computer memory is taken care of by tiny electrical circuits within the computer itself; long-term memory is on a separate storage system, usually using a disk or tape, that records the info magnetically in much the same way that a tape recorder does. See "buffer," "disk," and "tape."

modem: Connects your terminal with the main computer over phone lines. Cheaper modems usually need a phone handset plugged into them; more expensive ones often do not need a separate phone set. More expensive modems usually communicate at a higher speed (baud rate), so the computer and terminal react more quickly to your commands. Cheap and expensive have become very relative terms lately. A modem with the capabilities of a $1000 modem of a few years ago may now cost you around $100.

monitor: A TV-type screen that displays the commands you've given to the computer and its replies. Actually, a monitor is technically different from a TV, but, as in the case of *main-frame*, *mini*, and *micro* in describing computers, only computer and electronics nuts get bent out of shape if you use the wrong word for a monitor.

n: en: an arbitrary measurement used by typesetters. It is approximately the width of the letter *n*.

nesting: Progressively indenting a series of subparagraphs.

number register:
Number registers are small files where the computer looks for values denoting the desired type size, line length, indentation distance, etc. The number registers contain certain default values that are used unless you change them.

offset, page: The left-side margin. Together with the line length, it determines the right-side margin.

option: Modifies a command.

oral tradition:
A phrase that, when used in a computer context, means "we don't know how to write a manual about it, so ask."

password: Your account is protected by a password to keep it relatively private. The system administrator can overide your password, but nobody else can.

personal computer:
Or microcomputer; it has the terminal and computer together at one spot. This was formerly called a home computer, before the computer companies gave up trying to figure out why people were using $10 pocket calculators instead of $1500 computers to balance their checkbooks.

phototypesetter: Produces typeset copy for books, pamphlets, and such.

pipe: A symbol (|) used to hook two commands together.

point: A typesetter's measurement refering to the size (height) of type. 1 point equals 1/72 inch.

printer: Like a heavy-duty typewriter without a keyboard. Hook it up to a computer and it will type for you, if you have the proper printer "drive table" available. See "printer drive table" to find out why.

printer code: Tells the computer which "printer drive table" to use when formatting text.

printer drive table: Translates the symbols within the computer for the printer to print out your file accurately.

.profile: A hidden file useful for customizing Unix to suit you. See **Chapter 10, Hidden Files**.

programs: Computer programs are excruciatingly explicit instructions telling the computer what to do, step by step, to carry out a command.

prompt: A symbol that tells you the computer is ready to accept a command from you. A Unix prompt is usually a $ or %.

refer: A bibliography system to sort and format your bibliographies. It can also be used to develop a database, an information storage system that can be searched for the entry you want.

remote system: If your terminal is connected to the main computer via a modem rather than a direct or hard-wire connection, you have a remote system.

RS232: A special socket on the terminal to connect it with a modem.

source: A command telling the computer to look through a file, usually to make it carry out any instructions contained there.

superscript: Text one half-line up from the rest of the text. Usually used for footnote numbers.

system administrator(s):
These are the people who are supposed to keep the system running smoothly, add new programs, and such. They should have whatever information you need to use the system but frequently don't; they should be sensitive to complaints, but frequently aren't. Many of them are computer programmers with no experience in managing and dealing with people. They often have a hard time thinking of the needs of nonprogramming computer users and they rarely ask. There has been a shakeup among computer companies; there will be a shakeup among computer system administrators soon. The good ones will survive, and we will be better off. Hopefully you have some good ones in your computer center already.

tape: Large computers often use tape for long-term memory storage because you can store a lot of data on a tape. Tape tends to be slower when you are looking for a file, so it's not as good as a disk for constant use, although some cheap computers have used cassette style tape instead of a disk. On a Unix system, files are generally ''dumped'' onto a tape periodically as a backup in case of accidental loss of disk-stored files because of malfunction, fire, flood, or assorted types of clumsiness.

TERM: TERM is shorthand for terminal and is usually used when you are telling the computer what type of terminal you are using so that it can adjust its responses.

terminal: A terminal usually consists of a keyboard, like a typewriter's, and a monitor or screen so that you can see the results of what you've typed. Some specialized (generally older) terminals simply type out what you've typed on a narrow sheet of paper, but they aren't very useful for most people.

unfillable space:
Use **\0**. Tells the computer that there should be a

space where this symbol appears while fooling it into treating two words as one word. Especially useful when sorting two word names.

Unix: Unix is an "operating system," a collection of programs that performs functions when you give it commands.

Unix computer system:
A computer system, Unix or any other, consists of a terminal and a computer, with modem and printer as optional equipment.

user documentation:
A dumb way of saying "manual."

vertical spacing:
Sets the space between lines. In standard **nroff** and **troff** it is usually set in units of lines, just as on a typewriter; when using the **-ms** macro package it is set in units of points, 12 points being the same as single space.

w: *who*; tells you who (login names) is using the computer you are on.

who: Use **w** or **who** to find out who is using the computer you are on.

Index